NEW DIRECTIONS FOR STUDENT SERVICES

John H. Schuh, *Iowa State University*
EDITOR-IN-CHIEF

Elizabeth J. Whitt, *University of Iowa*
ASSOCIATE EDITOR

Contemporary Financial Issues in Student Affairs

John H. Schuh
Iowa State University

EDITOR

Number 103, Fall 2003

D1404237

JOSSEY-BASS
San Francisco

CONTEMPORARY FINANCIAL ISSUES IN STUDENT AFFAIRS
John H. Schuh (ed.)
New Directions for Student Services, no. 103
John H. Schuh, Editor-in-Chief
Elizabeth J. Whitt, Associate Editor

Microfilm copies of issues and articles are available in 16mm and 35mm, as well as microfiche in 105mm, through University Microfilms Inc., 300 North Zeeb Road, Ann Arbor, Michigan 48106-1346.

ISSN 0164-7970   e-ISSN 1536-0695

NEW DIRECTIONS FOR STUDENT SERVICES is part of The Jossey-Bass Higher and Adult Education Series and is published quarterly by Wiley Subscription Services, Inc., A Wiley Company, at Jossey-Bass, 989 Market Street, San Francisco, California 94103-1741. Periodicals postage paid at San Francisco, California, and at additional mailing offices. Postmaster: Send address changes to New Directions for Student Services, Jossey-Bass, 989 Market Street, San Francisco, California 94103-1741.

New Directions for Student Services is indexed in College Student Personnel Abstracts and Contents Pages in Education.

SUBSCRIPTIONS cost $70.00 for individuals and $145.00 for institutions, agencies, and libraries. See ordering information page at end of book.

EDITORIAL CORRESPONDENCE should be sent to the Editor-in-Chief, John H. Schuh, N 243 Lagomarcino Hall, Iowa State University, Ames, Iowa 50011

Cover photograph by Wernher Krutein/PHOTOVAULT © 1990.

Jossey-Bass Web address: www.josseybass.com

CONTENTS

EDITOR'S NOTES

The financial situation in higher education, which has been challenging for at least the past decade, has continued to deteriorate in the past few years. State governmental support for public institutions has continued to erode, and most institutions have increased their reliance on tuition as a revenue source (National Center for Education Statistics, 2002). Student affairs units operate in this financial environment and have had to be nimble and creative to sustain their viability.

Typically, student affairs staff do not enter their profession because they seek to manage large budgets and other resources. In fact, often they would prefer to leave those chores to others (Woodard, Love, and Komives, 2000), although over the long term, not managing budgets effectively can result in serious problems for them. So this volume was conceived to provide a contemporary look at the financial challenges before student affairs and to provide recommendations, strategies, and solutions for the budgetary challenges that student affairs staff face.

This issue of *New Directions for Student Services* examines contemporary problems in selected areas of student affairs finance and hence should not be considered a compendium on the topic all by itself. Rather, this volume should be regarded as one of several in this series on managing resources in student affairs. Others that address related topics include Issue 89, *The Role Student Aid Plays in Enrollment Management* (Coomes, 2000); Issue 92, *Leadership and Management Issues for a New Century* (Woodard, Love, and Komives, 2000); Issue 96, *Developing External Partnerships for Cost-Effective, Enhanced Services* (Dietz and Enchelmayer, 2001); and Issue 101, *Planning and Achieving Successful Student Affairs Facilities Projects* (Price, 2003). Taken as a set, the five issues provide a comprehensive view of the resource management issues that student affairs offices on contemporary college campuses must address.

This volume looks at seven specific issues concerning the financing of student affairs on contemporary college campuses. In Chapter One, I provide an overview and a framework for the financial environment in higher education. Student affairs is not divorced from the overall financial environment, and this chapter provides background information about how the environment has evolved over time.

In Chapter Two, Joan Claar and Hazel Scott compare and contrast the financial environment of public and private institutions. They use a case study to illustrate the differences between these two types of institutions.

Tim Schroer and Chris Johnson identify and discuss some the challenges in providing financing for student unions and student activities in

NEW DIRECTIONS FOR STUDENT SERVICES, no. 103, Fall 2003 © Wiley Periodicals, Inc.

Chapter Three. As services and programs have expanded over the years, new financial challenges have arisen for professionals in these areas.

Rich Keeling and Dennis Heitzmann provide a detailed look at financing health and counseling services in Chapter Four. These areas are linked because they face many of the same financial issues, including the need to manage costs in a very difficult financial environment.

Student housing is the focus of Chapter Five, prepared by Mary Ann Ryan. The very nature of student housing has changed dramatically over the years, and this chapter covers such issues as technology infusion and renovation.

Howard Taylor, William Canning, Paul Brailsford, and Frank Rokosz look at contemporary issues in recreation finance in Chapter Six. The days when campus recreation consisted of intramural events are long over, and these authors provide a detailed look at how to develop a contemporary recreation program from a financial point of view.

I wrap up the volume in Chapter Seven with some ideas about how to demonstrate financial accountability in student affairs. With so many stakeholders interested in how resources are managed, student affairs officers must have a plan by which they can demonstrate that they are using resources wisely.

It is unlikely that financial challenges for student affairs officers will disappear in the foreseeable future. Hence it is important that strategies be developed to ensure that programs and services that serve students and other important stakeholders survive and thrive. Our hope is that this issue of *New Directions for Student Services* will encourage fruitful conversations about student affairs finance and that new and creative solutions can be identified in this challenging environment.

John H. Schuh
Editor

References

Coomes, M. D. (ed.). *The Role Student Aid Plays in Enrollment Management.* New Directions for Student Services, no. 89. San Francisco: Jossey-Bass, 2000.

Dietz, L. H., and Enchelmayer, E. J. (eds.). *Developing External Partnerships for Cost-Effective, Enhanced Services.* New Directions for Student Services, no. 96. San Francisco: Jossey-Bass, 2001.

National Center for Education Statistics. *Digest of Education Statistics, 2001.* Washington, D.C.: U.S. Department of Education, 2002.

Price, J. (ed.). *Planning and Achieving Successful Student Affairs Facilities Projects.* New Directions for Student Services, no. 101. San Francisco: Jossey-Bass, 2003.

Woodard, D. B., Jr., Love, P., and Komives, S. R. (eds.). *Leadership and Management Issues for a New Century.* New Directions for Student Services, no. 92. San Francisco: Jossey-Bass, 2000.

JOHN H. SCHUH *is distinguished professor and chair of the department of educational leadership and policy studies at Iowa State University. He was a student affairs practitioner for twenty-seven years.*

1

This chapter examines factors that influence higher education finance, trends in revenue and expenditures of institutions of higher education, and current strategies used to meet financial challenges.

The Financial Environment of Student Affairs

John H. Schuh

Woodard, Love, and Komives (2000) observed the following about the contemporary financial environment of student affairs: "The higher education woes of the past thirty years have challenged every sector of higher education to rethink long-term sources of funding for campus programs an activities" (p. 71). Various strategies have been employed to deal with this situation. Public colleges and universities have attempted to compensate with reductions in state government support by raising tuition and fees at accelerating rates (Institute for Higher Education Policy, 1999b). Private institutions, too, have raised their tuition and fee schedules at a rate higher than economic barometers such as the consumer price index (Clotfelter, 1996). Students, the primary focus of student affairs programs and activities, have been affected directly. Since financial aid programs have not kept pace with the cost of attendance at colleges and universities (Institute for Higher Education Policy, 1999a), many students have had to assume increasingly larger debt to attend college (Fossey, 1998). More students, at all income levels, are borrowing more money to attend college (National Center for Public Policy and Higher Education, 2002). From a policy perspective, serious questions are being raised about the extent to which students from modest economic backgrounds will have access to institutions of higher education in the future (Terenzini, Cabrera, and Bernal, 2001).

Student affairs units function in this environment. Student affairs has been conceived as providing programs that promote inclusiveness, celebrate differences (Brazzell and Reisser, 1999), and encourage student involvement outside the classroom (Kuh, Schuh and Whitt, 1991). But as more diverse students are admitted to institutions of higher education, student affairs practitioners will not only need to "expand their knowledge for working with these learners but also to find better and more cost effective methods for doing so" (Gibbs, 1999, p. 62). Without an appropriate resource base, student affairs units will be hard-pressed to fulfill their obligations to their campuses and students.

This chapter has been prepared to frame the economic environment in which institutions of higher education in general and divisions of student affairs in particular operate. First, attention will be directed toward selected trends of the general environment in which colleges and universities operate. Then revenues and expenditure trends will be examined. Finally, strategies that institutions are using to readjust their budgets to the financial environment will be identified. This information should provide a framework for subsequent chapters.

Selected Trends Affecting Student Affairs Finance

Several aspects of the contemporary environment have had a significant influence on the financial operations of student affairs. Five are discussed here: institutional mission, austerity, accountability, federal mandates, and technology.

Institutional Mission. Lyons (1993) observed that the mission of the institution is the "most important factor that determines the shape and substance of student affairs" (p. 14). Little has changed since that assertion was published. An institution's mission statement guides day-to-day practices and informs student affairs professionals as they develop policies and implement new programs (Barr, 2000). In addition, mission statements can be very helpful in determining how to adjust and shape programs. For example, as the composition of a student body changes, new programs might be initiated while other programs may have to be scaled back or eliminated. The influence of the institution's mission on student affairs operations is unlikely to diminish in the foreseeable future.

Austerity. One consequence of the challenging financial environment is austerity, which "causes legislatures, state coordinating boards, and even consolidated boards to look more critically at institutional roles, at the availability and distribution of functions and programs, at effectiveness, and at educational operational costs" (Berdahl and McConnell, 1999, p. 72). Barak and Kniker (2002) observed that higher education normally receives more careful scrutiny in difficult economic times, and the attention paid to the financial management of student affairs very well could be a consequence of the prevailing austere environment. As Reisser and Roper (1999, p. 114) asserted, "Increasing accountability to the public for educational outcomes, the need to cut costs, reduced funding from external sources, and declining enrollments on some campuses are among the innumerable pressing issues confronting education as leaders." The pressure to be more accountable has led to a more data-driven environment, in which assessment becomes an increasingly important activity.

Accountability and Assessment Activities. Assessment, according to Schuh and Upcraft (2001), is an activity that is undertaken for two reasons: accountability and improvement. Accountability takes into account such issues as linking planning goals and outcomes, meeting the needs of students, and providing evidence that learning goals have been achieved by the time students graduate. Implicit in all of these activities is the careful use of resources, which are limited and are likely to be scarce now and in the future.

An aspect of the assessment movement that has received increasing emphasis has been developing strategic indicators and engaging in benchmarking as an administrative practice. Taylor and Massy (1996) advocate the development of strategic indicators that "allow an institution to compare its position in key strategic areas to competitors, to past performance, or to goals set previously" (pp. xi–xii). Benchmarking, according to Bender and Schuh (2002, p. 1), is "one approach that higher education leaders can employ to measure the extent to which institutional goals and objectives are being met." Benchmarking is a way of demonstrating accountability to various constituencies and a way of shoring up what Blimling and Whitt (1999, p. 7) have called "waning confidence in higher education's ability to make a difference in the lives of students and society."

Federal Mandates. Woodard (2001) has identified a number of federal mandates that have had "serious budgetary implications" (p. 247). Among these are Title IX, the Family Educational Rights and Privacy Act (FERPA), the Americans with Disabilities Act and Section 504 of the Rehabilitation Act of 1973, and the Campus Security Act of 1990. Title IX bans discrimination on the basis of sex. What this means, in essence, is that opportunities ought to be equal for men and women. In intercollegiate athletics, this has had the effect of creating a number of intercollegiate sports teams for women, thereby engendering additional costs. FERPA has resulted in making additional information available to students and their families. The ADA and Section 504 have mandated that all services, programs, and facilities be made available to students who, in the years before the legislation was passed, may not have had access to such institutional opportunities. The Campus Security Act requires that certain kinds of information be shared with the campus community and reported to various stakeholders. These mandates, while laudable in their intent, have come without commensurate funding. So institutions have had to generate the funds to satisfy them. In some instances, student affairs has taken the lead on campus in meeting the requirements of the mandates.

Technology. Technology is another factor that has resulted in increasing costs. Upcraft and Goldsmith (2000) identified a number of ways that technology has influenced the work of student affairs, from career services Web pages to online applications for admission and financial aid to degree audit programs to be used in academic advising. All of this technology provides improved services for students, but Upcraft and Goldsmith point out that there is a potential for "economic bifurcation" on college campuses: "Those who had access to computers prior to college and those who can afford their own computers will have an edge over those who have no experience with computers prior to college and who cannot afford them" (2000, p. 223). In addition, the cost of providing contemporary computing equipment, fax machines, photocopiers, personal organizers, and other forms of technology represents a substantial investment that was not a budget consideration two decades ago. Not only is introducing technology to the workplace expensive, but keeping it up to date and making good decisions about strategically purchasing new technology are challenging and difficult activities.

Current Revenue and Expenditure Trends in Financing Higher Education

Among the most important strategic indicators for an institution of higher education are its revenue and expenditures structures (Taylor and Massy, 1996). Looking at these indicators, taken together, is a good way of understanding the financial health of a college or university. Let's take a look at the revenue and expenditures trends in higher education since 1980.

Revenues. The *Digest of Education Statistics,* published by the National Center for Education Statistics (NCES), reports revenue trends for higher education on an annual basis. In the most recent edition of the *Digest* (2002) at the time of this writing, two important revenue trends are apparent. First, tuition and fees, as sources of revenue, have grown increasingly important over the years. Taken in the aggregate, tuition and fees have grown from 21 percent of current funds revenue for degree-granting institutions in 1980–81 to 27.9 percent of revenues for degree-granting institutions in 1995–96. When just public institutions are considered, growth was from 12.9 percent of current funds revenue in 1980–81 to 19 percent in 1996–97. These data are reported in Table 1.1. Private institutions have also shown growth in their reliance on tuition and fees as an income source. In 1980–81, private not-for-profit institutions derived 35.9 percent of their income from tuition and fees. By 1995–96, the percentage had grown to 41.5. These data are presented in Table 1.2.

When one examines current fund revenue sources by Carnegie type for both public and private not-for-profit institutions, the difference in the range of dependence on tuition and fees as a revenue source is apparent. Some of the Carnegie types rely very heavily on tuition and fees, while others derive more income from other sources. The range for public institutions in 1996–97 was from 15.47 percent of income for Research II universities (using the Carnegie typology at the time) to 31 percent for baccalaureate institutions. These data are presented in Table 1.3. Private not-for-profit institutions rely even more heavily on tuition and fees than their

Table 1.1. Percentage of Current Fund Revenues Derived from Various Sources for Public Degree-Granting Institutions of Higher Education, Selected Years, 1980–1997

Source	1980–81	1985–86	1990–91	1992–93	1993–94	1994–95	1995–96	1996–97
Tuition and fees	12.9	14.5	16.1	18.0	18.4	18.4	18.8	19.0
Federal government	12.8	10.5	10.3	10.8	11.0	11.1	11.1	11.0
State governments	45.6	45.0	40.3	36.8	35.9	35.9	35.8	35.6
Local governments	3.8	3.6	3.7	3.7	4.0	4.0	4.1	3.9
Private gifts, grants, contracts	2.5	3.2	3.8	4.0	4.0	4.0	4.1	4.3
Endowment income	.5	.6	.5	.6	.6	.6	.6	.6
Sales and services	19.6	20.0	22.7	23.4	23.4	23.1	22.2	22.2
Other sources	2.4	2.6	2.6	2.7	2.7	3.1	3.3	3.3

Source: National Center for Education Statistics, 2001, tab. 328.

Table 1.2. Percentage of Current Revenues Derived from Various Sources by Private Not-for-Profit Degree-Granting Institutions of Higher Education, Selected Years, 1980–1996

Source	1980–81	1985–86	1990–91	1991–92	1992–93	1993–94	1994–95	1995–96
Tuition and fees	35.9	37.8	39.4	39.7	40.2	40.9	41.4	41.5
Federal government	19.0	16.8	15.7	15.6	15.2	14.8	14.7	14.1
State governments	1.9	2.0	2.3	2.5	2.3	2.0	2.1	1.9
Local governments	.8	.6	.7	.7	.7	.8	.6	.7
Private gifts, grants, contracts	5.0	5.2	4.1	3.9	4.1	4.2	4.2	4.6
Endowment income	5.2	5.4	5.3	4.9	4.8	4.7	4.8	5.3
Sales and services	23.5	23.7	23.3	23.7	23.6	23.7	22.6	21.6
Other sources	4.2	4.4	4.5	4.5	4.5	4.4	4.8	5.4

Source: National Center for Education Statistics, 2001, tab. 330.

public counterparts do. The range for these institutions is from 13.1 percent of income resulting from tuition and fees to 53.5 percent of income for master's institutions. These data are given in Table 1.4.

Expenditures. This discussion is framed by the definitions of student services used by the Integrated Postsecondary Education Data System (IPEDS). *Student services,* according to the NCES (2001), is defined as "funds expended for admissions, registrar activities, and activities whose primary purpose is to contribute to students' emotional and physical well-being and to their intellectual, cultural, and social development outside the context of the formal instructional program. Examples are career guidance, counseling, financial aid administration, and student health services (except when operated as a self-supporting auxiliary enterprise). Include the administrative allowance for Pell Grants."

Expenditures for student services, according to the NCES, have been remarkably stable from 1980–81 through 1996–97. For public

Table 1.3. Percentage Distribution of Current Fund Revenues for Public Degree-Granting Institutions, by Source of Funds and Institutional Type, 1996–97

Source	Tuition and Fees	Federal Government	State Government	Local Government	Private Gifts and Grants	Endowment Earnings	Educational Activities	Auxiliary Enterprises	Hospitals	Other Current Income
Research I	15.47	14.68	28.03	.48	6.42	1.03	4.38	10.13	16.59	2.79
Research II	23.95	11.03	39.58	.22	5.38	.82	3.19	13.11	0.00	2.72
Doctoral	23.44	8.48	41.94	.68	4.73	.75	2.21	11.72	.07	5.96
Master's	27.55	5.74	45.74	.61	2.14	.23	1.78	12.76	1.11	2.33
Baccalaureate	31.00	6.99	42.72	.75	2.58	.21	1.46	12.01	0.00	2.29
Associate of Arts	21.36	5.29	43.69	18.87	1.04	.08	.72	5.85	0.00	3.10

Source: National Center for Education Statistics, 2001, tab. 332.

Table 1.4. Percentage Distribution of Current Fund Revenues for Private Degree-Granting Institutions, by Source of Funds and Institutional Type, 1996–97

Source	Research I	Research II	Doctoral	Master's	Baccalaureate	Associate of Arts
Tuition and fees	13.1	24.0	43.8	53.5	36.3	46.7
Federal appropriations	0	0	0	0.7	0.1	0.1
State appropriations	0.2	0.1	0.4	0.5	0.2	0.4
Local appropriations	0	0	0	0	0	0
Federal grants and contracts	13.4	6.1	5.1	3.5	2.3	5.5
State grants and contracts	0.5	0.6	1.2	0.9	0.8	1.8
Local grants and contracts	0.6	0	0.2	0.1	0	0.1
Private gifts and grants	10.5	12.5	11.1	11.5	15	15.6
Investment return	28.8	29.2	16.3	13.6	29.4	11
Educational activities	3.9	0.3	4.4	0.7	0.5	1.5
Auxiliary enterprises	4.8	10.8	8.8	11.9	12.4	8.0
Hospitals, independent operations, and other	24.1	16.4	8.8	3.2	2.1	9.9

Source: National Center for Education Statistics, 2001, tab. 333.

degree-granting institutions, 4.6 percent of current fund expenditures were spent on student services in 1980–81. This grew to 5.0 percent in 1996–97. These data are presented in Table 1.5. Private degree-granting institutions spent similar percentages of their budgets on student services. In 1980–81, these institutions spent 4.4 percent of their expenditures on student services. By 1995–96, this figure had grown to 5.4 percent. These data are presented in Table 1.6.

As was the case with revenues, institutional type has an effect on the percentage of expenditures for student services. In 1996–97, the range for public degree-granting institutions was from 2.51 percent of current funds expenditures for Research I institutions to 9.84 percent at associate of arts degree-granting institutions. In terms of the actual range of dollars spent in 1996–97, baccalaureate institutions spent the least, on average ($744 per student), on student services, whereas doctoral universities spent the most ($861 per student) on student services. These data are provided in Table 1.7

Private Research I universities spent the smallest percentage of budget in 1996–97 on student services (2.9 percent), while private associate of arts institutions spent the most, 16.3 percent of their budget, on student services in 1996–97. But when the percentages are converted to dollars spent per full-time-equivalent student, a slightly different picture emerges. In actual dollars, associate of arts institutions spent the most per student, $2,517, while Research II universities spent the least, $1,390 per student. These data are summarized in Table 1.8.

One other pattern worth noting emerges from these data. On average and regardless of Carnegie type, private institutions spent more money per

Table 1.5. Percentage of Current Fund Expenditures of Public Degree-Granting Institutions, by Purpose, 1980–1997

Purpose	1980–81	1985–86	1990–91	1991–92	1992–93	1993–94	1994–95	1995–96	1996–97
Instruction	35.1	34.5	33.7	33.2	32.8	32.6	32.6	32.3	32.1
Research	9.0	9.0	10.1	10.1	10.1	10.2	10.2	10.1	10.1
Public service	4.1	4.0	4.3	4.3	4.4	4.3	4.4	4.5	4.6
Academic support	7.2	7.4	7.5	7.4	7.3	7.4	7.3	7.5	7.5
Student services	4.6	4.6	4.7	4.7	4.9	4.9	4.9	4.9	5.0
Institutional support	8.4	9.0	8.6	8.5	8.7	8.5	8.6	9.0	9.0
Physical plant	8.7	8.2	7.2	6.9	6.8	6.8	6.6	6.7	6.6
Scholarships and fellowships	2.5	2.5	2.9	3.3	3.6	3.9	4.0	4.3	4.4
Mandatory transfers	1.2	1.2	1.1	1.1	1.1	1.1	1.2	1.2	1.2
Auxiliary enterprises	11.0	10.8	9.7	9.7	9.6	9.7	9.7	9.5	9.6
Hospitals	8.0	8.5	10.0	10.6	10.6	10.4	10.2	9.9	9.6
Independent operations	0.2	0.2	0.2	0.2	0.2	0.2	0.2	0.2	0.2

Source: National Center for Education Statistics, 2001, tab. 343.

Table 1.6. Percentage of Current Fund Expenditures of Private Degree-Granting Institutions, by Purpose, 1980–1997

Purpose	1980–81	1985–86	1990–91	1991–92	1992–93	1993–94	1994–95	1995–96	1996–97
Instruction	27.0	26.6	26.4	26.6	26.5	26.5	26.7	26.8	27.0
Research	8.5	8.0	8.1	7.7	7.5	7.7	7.7	7.8	7.7
Public service	1.6	1.8	2.0	2.0	2.1	2.3	2.3	2.5	2.4
Academic support	5.7	5.7	5.9	5.9	5.8	5.7	5.7	5.7	6.1
Student services	4.4	4.8	4.8	4.9	4.9	4.9	5.1	5.4	5.1
Institutional support	10.1	10.7	10.6	10.7	10.6	10.2	10.3	10.2	10.6
Physical plant	7.7	7.1	6.4	6.2	6.1	6.1	6.1	6.0	6.1
Scholarships and fellowships	6.6	7.5	8.7	9.2	10.1	10.6	11.0	11.3	11.4
Mandatory transfers	1.4	1.3	1.5	1.4	1.4	1.4	1.4	1.6	1.4
Auxiliary enterprises	12.1	10.8	10.1	9.8	9.3	9.1	9.0	8.8	8.9
Hospitals	9.4	9.7	9.3	9.4	9.9	9.8	9.7	9.3	8.5
Independent operations	5.5	6.0	6.1	5.9	5.8	5.6	5.0	4.9	4.6

Source: National Center for Education Statistics, 2001, tab. 344.

Table 1.7. Expenditures of Public Institutions per Full-Time-Equivalent Student, by Purpose and Institutional Type, 1996–97 ($)

Purpose	Research I	Research II	Doctoral	Master's	Baccalaureate	Associate of Arts
Total educational and general	24,020	16,226	15,481	9,755	7,543	7,180
Instruction	8,085	5,945	5,837	4,337	3,039	3,403
Research	5,876	2,797	1,758	325	119	8
Public service	1,895	1,294	937	359	282	175
Academic support	2,332	1,732	1,636	950	792	619
Student services	817	764	861	785	744	754
Institutional support	1,609	1,330	2,090	1,208	1,074	1,143
Operation and maintenance of plant	1,550	1,163	1,135	920	785	725
Scholarships and fellowships	1,394	973	992	697	570	290
Mandatory transfers	463	229	235	175	140	64
Auxiliary enterprises	3,213	2,568	2,270	1,458	1,089	466
Hospitals	5,216	0	29	125	0	0
Independent operations	62	4	0	7	0	18

Source: National Center for Education Statistics, 2001, tab. 340.

Table 1.8. Expenditures of Private Not-for-Profit Institutions per Full-Time-Equivalent Student, by Purpose and Institutional Type, 1996–97 ($)

Purpose	Research I	Research II	Doctoral	Master's	Baccalaureate	Associate of Arts
Total expenditures	79,240	30,398	23,803	14,494	17,141	15,490
Instruction	21,288	10,096	8,721	5,452	5,748	5,115
Research	14,776	2,956	1,454	247	146	103
Public service	1,819	305	1,101	227	125	71
Academic support	4,878	1,795	2,839	1,286	1,339	819
Student services	2,267	1,390	1,579	1,641	2,053	2,517
Institutional support	5,588	3,483	3,688	2,452	2,998	2,777
Operation and maintenance of plant	562	665	548	532	827	1,065
Scholarships and fellowships	527	565	559	462	880	554
Auxiliary enterprises	5,739	4,382	2,691	2,010	2,900	1,325
Hospitals and independent operations	21,796	5,301	623	184	124	1,145

Source: National Center for Education Statistics, 2001, tab. 341.

student on student services than public institutions did. This is true for other expense categories as well. In the final analysis, private institutions simply have more money to work with than their public counterparts do, the implications of which have been analyzed by Alexander (2001), who asserts that a two-tiered system of higher education may be resulting from this phenomenon. Without question, what emerges from his data are two tiers of compensation for faculty.

Selected Strategies to Address the Financial Climate

A number of strategies have been adopted by colleges and universities to address their financial problems. We shall examine several of them.

Using a Cost-Centered Approach to Budgeting. In this approach, a unit is thought of as its own revenue and expenditure center. In short, every unit or department "pays its own way" (Woodard, 2001, p. 261). This works best with auxiliary services, such as student housing or the campus bookstore, but it can be applied to other units in student affairs, such as health services, counseling centers, or other units that generate their own revenues. A variation of this type of budgeting is responsibility-centered budgeting, which makes each academic or service unit "financially responsible for its own activities" (p. 262). While this approach assigns responsibility to each unit for its financial health, it can also place units in competition with one another for resources on campus.

Cost-centered or responsibility-centered budgeting can be adopted simultaneously with the second strategy, moving various student affairs units off the campus general fund, defined as the tuition that students pay at private institutions or tuition plus state appropriations at public institutions.

Reducing Student Affairs Dependence on General Fund Revenues. Recognizing that there is wide latitude in how institutions define their "general fund," moving student affairs units from being funded by the campus general fund to dedicated student fees and fees for service is an approach that many institutions use. As noted, this approach is often adopted in concert with taking a cost-centered or responsibility-centered budgeting approach. In practical terms, this might mean that a counseling center would be funded by a dedicated fee that all students would pay each semester and that additional fees would be charged to users of the center, perhaps after a certain number of free visits. The same approach could be used at health centers, where visits to see health care providers would be provided without charge, but students would be charged for laboratory or pharmacy services.

Outsourcing and Privatization. Outsourcing and privatization are other trends that are affecting student affairs specifically and higher education in general. Palm (2001) has identified a number of reasons that institutions are engaged in these activities, including to reduce costs, to free up resources for other purposes, and to obtain resources not available internally. Monetta and Dillon (2001, p. 31) conclude that "it is common, and in many cases desirable, to convey management responsibility for some campus services to a private partner when the benefits derived from the relationship outweigh the risks of continued self-operation or when the partnership is likely to enhance service quality or reduce costs." Outsourcing and privatization provide different opportunities and challenges for student affairs leaders who administer these relationships with off-campus vendors. These trends are likely to continue in the future.

A variation of the theme of developing partnerships with off-campus entities is described by Askew (2001). She identified a number of partnerships that were formed by campus organizations and programs with off-campus organizations to enrich and enhance the experience for students and community members. Among these are the America Reads program at the University of Illinois at Urbana-Champaign, the Bridge to Hope program at the University of Hawaii, and the Blackburn Institute at the University of Alabama at Tuscaloosa.

Fundraising. Fundraising is an activity that developed as a consequence to the tightening financial situation of higher education and is a potential source of additional revenues for specific initiatives in student affairs. Jackson (2000, p. 610) observed that "student affairs programs now have the opportunity to help their institution finance projects that may not have been funded by external sources a decade ago." He adds that student affairs staff should gain support for programs similar to the approach taken in academic affairs.

A Final Word

The financial environment in which colleges and universities function has been challenging for a number of years and is unlikely to change in the foreseeable future. As a consequence, student affairs leaders will have to be creative and bold in their approach to generating adequate resources to underwrite their programs, services, and learning experiences in the future.

References

Alexander, F. K. "The Silent Crisis: The Relative Fiscal Capacity of Public Universities to Compete for Faculty." *Review of Higher Education,* 2001, *24,* 113–129.

Askew, P. E. "The University as a Source for Community and Academic Partnerships." In L. H. Dietz and E. J. Enchelmayer (eds.), *Developing External Partnerships for Cost-Effective, Enhanced Service.* New Directions for Student Services, no. 96. San Francisco: Jossey-Bass, 2001.

Barak, R. J., and Kniker, C. R. "Benchmarking by State Higher Education Boards." In B. E. Bender and J. H. Schuh (eds.), *Using Benchmarking to Inform Practice in Higher Education.* New Directions for Higher Education, no. 118. San Francisco: Jossey-Bass, 2002.

Barr, M. J. "The Importance of the Institutional Mission." In M. J. Barr, M. K. Desler, and Associates, *The Handbook of Student Affairs Administration.* (2nd ed.) San Francisco: Jossey-Bass, 2000.

Bender, B. E., and Schuh, J. H. "Editor's Notes." In B. E. Bender and J. H. Schuh (eds.), *Using Benchmarking to Inform Practice in Higher Education.* New Directions for Higher Education, no. 118. San Francisco: Jossey-Bass, 2002.

Berdahl, R. O., and McConnell, T. R. "Autonomy and Accountability: Who Controls Academe?" In P. G Altbach, R. O. Berdahl, and P. J. Gumport (eds.), *American Higher Education in the Twenty-First Century.* Baltimore: Johns Hopkins University Press, 1999.

Blimling, G. S., and Whitt, E. J. "Identifying the Principles That Guide Student Affairs Practice." In G. S. Blimling, E. J. Whitt, and Associates, *Good Practice in Student Affairs*. San Francisco: Jossey-Bass, 1999.

Brazzell, J. C., and Reisser, L. "Creating Inclusive Communities. " In G. S. Blimling, E. J. Whitt, and Associates. *Good Practice in Student Affairs*. San Francisco: Jossey-Bass, 1999.

Clotfelter, C. T. *Buying the Best: Cost Escalation in Elite Higher Education*. Princeton, N.J.: Princeton University Press, 1996.

Fossey, R. "The Dizzying Growth of the Federal Student Loan Program." In R. Fossey and M. Bateman (eds.), *Condemning Students to Debt: College Loans and Public Policy*. New York: Teachers College Press, 1998.

Gibbs, A. "Changing Government Roles Relative to Higher Education." In C. S. Johnson and H. E. Cheatham (eds.), *Higher Education Trends for the Next Century: A Research Agenda for Student Success*. Washington, D.C.: American College Personnel Association, 1999.

Institute for Higher Education Policy. *State of Diffusion: Defining Student Aid in an Era of Multiple Purposes*. Washington, D.C.: Institute for Higher Education Policy, 1999a.

Institute for Higher Education Policy. *The Tuition Puzzle: Putting the Pieces Together*. Washington, D.C.: Institute for Higher Education Policy, 1999b.

Jackson, M. L. "Fundraising and Development. " In M. J. Barr, M. K. Desler, and Associates, *The Handbook of Student Affairs Administration*. (2nd ed.) San Francisco: Jossey-Bass, 2000.

Kuh, G. D., Schuh, J. H., and Whitt, E. J. *Involving Colleges*. San Francisco: Jossey-Bass, 1991.

Lyons, J. L. "The Importance of Institutional Mission." In M. J. Barr and Associates, *The Handbook of Student Affairs Administration*. San Francisco: Jossey-Bass, 1993.

Monetta, L., and Dillon, W. L. "Strategies for Effective Outsourcing." In L. H. Dietz and E. J. Enchelmayer (eds.), *Developing External Partnerships for Cost-Effective, Enhanced Service*. New Directions for Student Services, no. 96. San Francisco: Jossey-Bass, 2001.

National Center for Education Statistics. "Web-Based Data Collection Screens, 2001–02." 2001. [http://nces.ed.gov/ipeds/survey2001.asp].

National Center for Education Statistics. *Digest of Education Statistics, 2000*. Washington, D.C.: National Center for Education Statistics, 2001. [http://nces.ed.gov/pubs2002/digest2001].

National Center for Public Policy and Higher Education. *Losing Ground: A National Status Report on the Affordability of American Higher Education*. San Jose, Calif.: National Center for Public Policy and Higher Education, 2002.

Palm, R. L. "Partnering Through Outsourcing." In L. H. Dietz and E. J. Enchelmayer (eds.), *Developing External Partnerships for Cost-Effective, Enhanced Service*. New Directions for Student Services, no. 96. San Francisco: Jossey-Bass, 2001.

Reisser, L., and Roper, L. D. "Using Resources to Achieve Institutional Missions and Goals." In G. S. Blimling and E. J. Whitt (eds.), *Good Practice in Student Affairs: Principles to Foster Student Learning*. San Francisco: Jossey-Bass, 1999.

Schuh, J. H., and Upcraft, M. L. *Assessment Practice in Student Affairs*. San Francisco: Jossey-Bass, 2001.

Taylor, B. E., and Massy, W. F. *Strategic Indicators for Higher Education*. Princeton, N.J.: Peterson, 1996.

Terenzini, P. T., Cabrera, A. F., and Bernal, E. M. *Swimming Against the Tide: The Poor in American Higher Education*. New York: College Entrance Examination Board, 2001.

Upcraft, M. L., and Goldsmith, H. "Technological Changes in Student Affairs Administration." In M. J. Barr and Associates, *The Handbook of Student Affairs Administration*. San Francisco: Jossey-Bass, 2000.

Woodard, D. B., Jr. "Finance and Budgeting." In R. B. Winston Jr. and others, *The Professional Student Affairs Administrator*. Bristol, Pa.: Taylor & Francis, 2001.
Woodard, D. B., Jr., Love, P., and Komives, S. R. (eds.). *Leadership and Management Issues for a New Century*. New Directions for Student Services, no. 92. San Francisco: Jossey-Bass, 2000.

JOHN H. SCHUH *is distinguished professor and chair of the department of educational leadership and policy studies at Iowa State University. He was a student affairs practitioner for twenty-seven years.*

*The authors compare and contrast financial issues in
public and private colleges and universities. A case study
illustrates the financial environments in which these types
of institutions operate.*

Comparing Financial Issues in Public and Private Institutions

Joan M. Claar, Hazel J. Scott

As the costs of attending institutions of higher education increase, it is important to understand funding for both private and public institutions and the influence of the financial environment on students and on student affairs. This chapter reviews funding sources for private and public institutions, compares and contrasts the details of funding public and private higher education, and considers the implications for student affairs.

Colleges and universities, both public and private, come in a variety of sizes and with a variety of missions. Although many private colleges are small and most public institutions are large, there are numerous exceptions in both directions. For the purpose of this discussion, however, private colleges will be assumed to be small institutions with five thousand or fewer students, and public institutions will be assumed to have enrollments in excess of five thousand students. The intent is not to ignore institutions that do not fit these assumptions but rather to provide a framework to aid the discussion of financial issues in student affairs in all institutions.

Sources for funding private and public colleges and universities will be reviewed in terms of how the annual budget is determined; the place of student affairs in budget planning; the impact of enrollment, fundraising, and tuition in good and poor economic times; and the role played by institutional governance in budgeting priorities. Two case studies are presented: one of a small, private liberal arts institution and one of a large urban state university. The differences and similarities between public and private institutions and the impact of each on student affairs will be illustrated through the cases, and implications of the differences and similarities of financial issues in private and public institutions will be summarized.

NEW DIRECTIONS FOR STUDENT SERVICES, no. 103, Fall 2003 © Wiley Periodicals, Inc.

Private Colleges and Universities

The process of developing the annual budget in private institutions varies significantly from one institution to another. Funding for private higher education generally comes from a combination of tuition and fees, room and board, gifts, and endowment income. The proportion of funding from each of those sources varies considerably from institution to institution, depending on the stability of enrollment as well as on the size of endowment and annual giving.

Tuition is the primary source of income for most private colleges. Although some small private colleges have large endowments that account for half (or even more) of their annual income, many others are dependent on tuition for more than half of the institutional income, and for some, tuition represents 90 percent or more of their income.

Some private institutions establish mandatory fees for areas such as health service, student activities, technology, and athletics; other institutions include in tuition everything except room and board. Because of the dependence on tuition income for funding, enrollment can have a dramatic impact on the annual budget. If fewer students enroll than were budgeted, the amount of room, board, and tuition for each projected student who did not enroll has to be deducted from the income after the academic year has started. If enrollments are greater than projected, the institution has more money for expenses than was budgeted.

Many private colleges are residential, and room and board is an additional source of both income and expense. Some private colleges use any income that exceeds room and board costs to balance the budget, while others establish a plant fund that is used for renovation and replacement in residence halls.

Endowment is a significant source of income for private colleges and universities. Generally, only a portion of the income from endowment is budgeted, and for some institutions, this can be used to enhance the programs and facilities as well as to maintain reasonable tuition rates. The annual fund, consisting of unrestricted gifts from alumni and friends during the year, is also an important source of income for many private institutions.

The governing boards of private institutions are ordinarily self-selected, with the existing board making new appointments. Those appointments are frequently made on the basis of the ability and willingness of the candidates to make significant financial contributions. The boards of private institutions have ultimate responsibility for the financial health of institutions and approve annual budgets.

Case 1: Private Residential College

John Dewey College, a private residential institution with an enrollment of approximately two thousand students, is located in a medium-sized midwestern city. Although enrollments have been stable, growth is not anticipated as a way of increasing institutional revenue. Student tuition income typically accounts for 75 percent of the college's annual income, with 24 percent coming from endowment income and annual gifts from alumni and friends of the institution and the remaining 1 percent coming from grants. It has long been a policy of the board of Dewey College not to charge additional fees for student services, activities, or facilities. The cost of attendance for students consists of tuition, room, and board.

During the past three years, the college has been engaged in institutional planning, with faculty, staff, administration, and students involved in the planning process. Priorities established for the near future through planning include enlivening campus life to enhance student involvement, improving and enriching the residential experience for students, enhancing the quality of the educational experience, planning and implementing a fundraising campaign to increase the financial viability of the college and minimize the size of tuition increases, and establishing a fund to improve and update campus facilities. It was anticipated that any new funding in the budget would be made available on the basis of the priorities established through the planning process.

Dewey College starts working on the next fiscal year's budget during late fall, and the president must make a recommendation regarding the level of tuition to the board of trustees at its January meeting. This fall, the vice president for finance reported to the president and her cabinet that due to a projected dip in enrollment and a reduction in endowment income resulting from a downturn in the economy, the projected income for the following year would be less than the current year's income. The vice president for finance projected a 3 percent decline in income for the next year.

In the budget proposal for priority funding in student affairs, the student union currently under construction is scheduled to open in the fall, and the cost of staffing the building and of utilities will add $1.5 million to the operating budget; the football field requires immediate resodding at a cost of approximately $200,000; a full-time assistant coaching position is scheduled to be added for women's basketball in order to address the issue of equity between men's and women's teams; and the residence halls require $50,000 for basic repairs, renovation, and furniture replacement. Academic affairs needs faculty positions to support a growing two-year-old academic program, funds to devote to technology support for the classroom, and funding for a critical new recruiting initiative in admissions. Institutional advancement is preparing to embark on a major, multimillion-dollar campaign that requires the addition of staff members at a cost of $300,000. In addition, a minimal salary increase for faculty and staff would add another $1 million to the budget. The initial projections for next year of having less income and new cost priorities totaling approximately $3.5 million resulted in the need to start the budget planning process with a reduction of 5 percent from the amount budgeted for the current year.

The president asked that the College Planning Committee (CPC), under the leadership of the vice president for finance, hold budget hearings and make recommendations to her for a balanced budget. Each vice president and the president made budget presentations to the CPC regarding the budget proposal for his or her division or office and the cuts that would be necessary in order to reach the 5 percent goal. In spite of reductions by some divisions that exceeded the required 5 percent, the proposed budget was not balanced at the end of the process because of the new costs. The committee, which included the college's vice presidents, then started the difficult task of determining which of the costs could not be delayed, such as the opening of the new building, and which costs could be delayed for a year. At the end of the process, the proposed budget was in balance, and there was a consensus on the priorities that would be addressed if there was more income than projected in next year's budget or in budget planning for the follow ing year.

The process described included student affairs as a full participant. Everyone participating gave up something that was deemed important in his or her division, and all divisions were given consideration for priorities that had been set by the planning committee for their areas. Programs had to be eliminated in order to provide funding for new priorities. For example, the elimination of men's wrestling and women's field hockey helped make available some funds to devote to the assistant coach for women's basketball and resodding the football field.

Although staff in the areas affected by the reductions were not enthusiastic about them, the process resulted in a strong commitment by everyone involved in the budgeting process to support the reductions. In addition, those who served on the CPC went away from the process with a far better understanding and appreciation for other divisions within the college, as well as for the institution's future financial needs.

Public Colleges and Universities

The budget process of public colleges and universities is determined both by the state and by the institution. The public process begins with an allocation from the state legislature based on the state's funding formula. This formula usually includes such factors as faculty workload, student enrollment, physical plant (buildings, custodial, repairs, utilities, and so on), and legislative program initiatives. Enrollment increases by level and by discipline can determine the student-faculty ratio and hence new faculty positions, administrative positions, and library volumes. The legislature-determined higher education allocations are then distributed to the individual institutions by a state higher education board. This board works with the state office of higher education, and both offices coordinate their activities with the state legislature and governor.

The roles of state governing boards vary by state, but all such boards have fiduciary responsibility for the financial management of the state system. Some states have separate boards for various types of institutions (for example, research institutions, regional institutions, and community colleges), while others have a single statewide coordinating board. They work with the state higher education office to determine funding priorities, set policy, and approve tuition and student fee rates.

The funding sources for public colleges and universities come from a combination of tuition, student fees, gifts, endowment income, and state and federal research grants. The proportion of funding from these sources varies by institutional mission, enrollment, size of endowment, and grant success.

Case 2: An Urban State University

Alpha State University is located in a large metropolitan city and has an enrollment of sixteen thousand students: twelve thousand undergraduates and four thousand graduate students. The university has experienced growth in some funding source areas: an enrollment growth of approximately 2 percent each year for the past two years, an increase in research dollars, and an increase in gift income. These increases reflect the institution's mission of recognition as a primary regional research center and its priorities for the past few years.

The university has a budget of $210 million. Some 55 percent of its budget, $115.5 million, comes from the state and is based on the state formula and also includes a state urban study initiative of $1 million. The second largest source of income comes from grants and contracts, representing 30 percent of the budget at $63 million. All students pay student fees. Students participate in determining the fees through a committee process. The fees pay for some student affairs staff, facilities, and programs. The fee is $390 per student, or 3 percent of the budget. The remaining 12 percent comes from gifts, endowments, and anticipated enrollment increases that are expected to continue the rate of growth of the past few years.

Alpha State University has a budget process that reflects the shared governance philosophy of higher education. It is multidimensional and representative of all segments of the institution (Woodard, 2001).

The university engaged in a planning process two years ago that led to a strategic plan with a written action plan. The university senate maintains a standing strategic planning committee that reviews the strategic plan annually and updates the action plan. By policy, the committee is composed of faculty, staff, administration, and students; 50 percent of its members are faculty. The vice president of academic affairs chairs the committee. The plans are approved by the university senate and are used to gauge institutional effectiveness and funding priorities.

The legislative budgeting process begins in January when it convenes for the new session, and the state governing board approves the institution's budget at its April meeting. The university begins its process in November when the university budget committee, chaired by the vice president for academic affairs, forwards a request to each college and major noninstructional unit of the university for new funding initiatives. The budget requests are due in January. This committee has a representative membership that includes as standing members the vice president for finance and administration, three deans, two students, two staff members, ten faculty, and one additional rotating senior administrator, which this year happens to be the vice president for student affairs.

The budget committee meets regularly to monitor the university's current-year budget and the tax revenue collection reports from the state budget office. Due to enrollment increases, the current budget projections are in the black, but because of the downturn in the economy, the state tax collections are down 3 percent for the second consecutive quarter. The vice president for finance and administration recommends proceeding cautiously for the next fiscal year in anticipation of budget reductions. The vice president for academic affairs agrees but philosophically believes that the university should fund its priorities even in tight fiscal years. The committee develops a process of internal reallocation (Barr, 2002).

The internal reallocation process requires each college and noninstructional unit to contribute a portion of its state funds to the budgeting process. From these funds, the budget committee will redirect funds to the priorities of the university. The funding priorities are determined by the strategic and action plans. The priorities are instruction, program effectiveness and centrality to the mission, and enrollment support.

Several units requested funds for new initiatives. The budget committee asked each vice president and college dean to present proposals for his or her respective unit. Academic affairs requested new faculty positions in business to support enrollment increases in the nationally ranked international business program ($250,000), funding for equipment in the hard sciences to enhance the generation of research grants ($500,000), and a position to support the new data system in enrollment services ($75,000). Student affairs submitted a proposal for a new position to meet Americans with Disabilities Act (ADA) requirements for a growing disabled student population ($75,000). Institutional advancement submitted a reorganization plan to initiate the $500 million capital campaign that demonstrated a need for additional staff members ($150,000). Finance and administration requested additional police officers to address a growing on-campus crime rate ($100,000).

In March, the state legislature approved the state budget, and the governor signed the budget, which required all state agencies to reduce their budgets for the next fiscal year by 6 percent. The state higher education governing board met to review the state allocation and to approve institutional budgets for the school system. In its deliberations, it approved a tuition increase of 4 percent and student activity fee increase of 9 percent for Alpha State.

The allocation for the university reflected increases for enrollment growth of the past year and for workload production. With a projected

3 percent increase in enrollment, it would also benefit from the tuition and student activity fee increases. The student activity fee funds some student services, health center, and day care center personnel, the student center facility, the recreation center facility, and general student activities. The approved fee increase was designated for student activities and increased services in the health center. The fee is a nonstate fund and not subject to state-imposed reductions.

The budget committee met to discuss ways to absorb the 6 percent reduction, fund some new initiatives, and balance the university's budget. The colleges and the noninstructional units were asked to prepare reductions of 4 and 6 percent, respectively. This would allow the university to balance its budget and fund $500,000 of new initiatives. In this scenario, a unit's net reduction could range from 3 to 8 percent, depending on the size of the original budget and any funded new initiative. The committee considered such factors as meeting the instructional needs of the growing enrollments, increasing effective research programs, potential sources of external funding, and essential services.

It was determined that the student affairs request was worthy of funding, but the committee thought that the proposal for an ADA position might be funded externally by the student activity fee. With the support of the student member of the budget committee, the vice president for student affairs presented this request to the student activity fee committee. The presentation focused on the new approved fees and the projected revenue increased from enrollment growth that would more than pay for the position. The position was approved for funding.

The president agreed to provide institutional advancement with seed money from his discretionary account to fund one position with the agreement that the position would become self-supporting within one year. In subsequent years, the position had development goals that exceeded the cost of the position and increased the university's endowment.

The committee redirected funds to academic affairs to partially support its request for new faculty and equipment. The vice president for academic affairs will determine the allocations.

All segments of the university participated in this representative process, and student affairs was at the table at all decision points. The outcome produced a balanced budget in which all instructional and noninstructional units participated through reductions and new initiatives. The budget committee recommended the budget to the president for approval in May. The budget positioned the university to advance its mission.

Alpha State University was able to lessen the impact of the state-imposed 6 percent budget reduction thanks to several factors: enrollment management that produced growth for two consecutive years, which resulted in increased state formula funding; projected enrollment growth for next year, which will result in increased tuition dollars; and increases in the student activity fee and university gifts, which provide flexibility.

In large public colleges and universities, the process is long by necessity. It involves both state and institutional processes. Both processes are collaborative and political, and the final result is negotiated. The legislature and governor are accountable to the people of the state, and the members of the budget committee are accountable to their respective constituency. Everyone is invested in the process and supports the outcome.

Comparing Private and Public Financing and Budgeting Procedures

Funding for private and public institutions varies by degree, as Table 2.1 illustrates. The two case studies indicated some of the sources of funding and the process for budgeting for both a private and a public institution of higher education. Certain common issues and concerns about finances exist among most, if not all, colleges and universities.

Similarities. *Securing Funding to Fulfill the Mission of the Institution.* Although the sources of funding and the procedures for budgeting may vary considerably in private and public higher education, the underlying issue is the same. All institutions work to obtain sufficient resources for fulfilling the mission of the institution, and the mission is the overarching philosophy driving the budget process (Barr, 2000). Clearly, this is not a simple process. Both case studies illustrated that there are many legitimate requests for budget additions, and the requests are funded on the basis of their relationship to the institutional mission and planning priorities. All institutions need a budget planning process that includes all divisions of the college or university and that allows each division to be heard and to have a say in the budgeting priorities.

Institutional Planning as a Basis for Budget Decisions. Institutional planning is common to both public and private institutions. Thoughtful and con-

Table 2.1. Percentage Comparison of Sources of Income, U.S. Public and Private Institutions of Higher Education

Income	Public (%)	Private (%)
Tuition and fees	19	42
Federal government	11.5	15
State government	37	3.5
Local government	6.8	2
Gifts, grants, contracts	5	12
Endowment income	4	6.7
Educational activities	11.8	12
Auxiliary enterprises	11.8	12
Hospitals	12.2	11.8
Other sources	4.9	7.3

Source: Adapted from the data of the National Center for Educational Statistics (1997), http://www.nces.ed.gov.

sidered decisions on budgeting are enhanced within a structured and coordinated planning process that is representative of all institutional constituents. The institutional plan can provide structure and priorities to budget discussions and decisions. The case studies demonstrate the commonality in process and outcome of planning. Both institutions had broad-based committees that included the chief student affairs officer and had planning documents establishing institutional priorities to guide decision making.

One of the priorities established by the planning committee at John Dewey College was to increase student involvement on campus. The decision to build a student union that requires an addition of $1.5 million to the annual budget for operating the building, the addition of an assistant women's basketball coach, and resodding the football field are all examples of funding planning priorities in student affairs. Alpha State University was successful in obtaining a new position to comply with ADA requirements because of its centrality to the institutional mission.

Realistic Tuition Rates. Tuition and fees have increased significantly over the past decade (Institute for Higher Education Policy, 1999), and since the early 1980s, tuition has increased annually at two to three times the rate of inflation (Upcraft, 1999). Table 2.2 illustrates the dramatic rise from 1976–77 to 1996–97. Keeping tuition at realistic rates is a shared concern by public and private institutions of higher education. The reasons are many, but of primary importance are public accountability and accessibility. Many institutions, both private and public, have a mission statement that includes accessibility of education to all who are academically eligible to attend the college or university. Data analyzed by Heller (1997) show that as prices rise, enrollments decline, even with the availability of financial aid. The cost of tuition has an impact on who can enroll and can also have an impact on the amount of time that matriculated students must work and the amount of time available for them to be on campus participating in academic and cocurricular activities. In setting tuition rates, policymakers have to consider federal financial aid policies, the institution-based scholarship program, economic trends, and educational costs.

Endowment, Annual Giving, and Grants and Contracts. The declining role of public revenues has increased the importance of endowment income, annual giving, and grants and contracts as revenue sources for both private and public institutions. The annual earnings from a sizable endowment can add stability to income and permit the institution to continue moving forward without charging current students the actual cost of education. Unrestricted annual giving can also provide an important boost to the annual budget. Both public and private institutions depend on these revenues as a significant source of support. Whereas some private schools rely on this revenue as a major source of funds, public institutions are becoming increasingly reliant on gifts.

Influence of the National Economy. The relationship between the national economy and institutional finances is an ongoing concern in both

Table 2.2. Average Tuition and Fees (in Dollars) by Type of Institution, 1980–2001

	Public University	Public Two-Year College	Private College	Public College	Private University
1980	840	355	3,020	662	3,811
1981	915	391	3,390	722	4,275
1982	1,042	434	3,853	813	4,887
1983	1,164	473	4,329	936	5,583
1984	1,284	528	4,726	1,052	6,217
1985	1,386	584	5,135	1,117	6,843
1986	1,536	641	5,641	1,157	7,374
1987	1,651	660	6,171	1,248	8,118
1988	1,726	706	6,574	1,407	8,771
1989	1,846	730	7,172	1,515	9,451
1990	2,035	756	7,778	1,608	10,348
1991	2,159	824	8,389	1,707	11,379
1992	2,409	936	9,060	1,931	12,037
1993	2,604	1,025	9,533	2,192	13,055
1994	2,820	1,125	10,100	2,360	13,874
1995	2,977	1,192	10,653	2,499	14,537
1996	3,151	1,239	11,297	2,660	15,605
1997	3,323	1,276	11,871	2,778	16,552
1998	3,486	1,314	12,338	2,877	17,229
1999	3,640	1,327	12,815	2,974	18,340
2000	3,768	1,338	13,361	3,091	19,307
2001	3,983	1,359	14,281	3,212	20,143

Adapted from the data of the National Center for Educational Statistics (1997), http://www.nces.ed.gov.

private and public institutions. The impact on state institutions is direct and immediate. A downturn in the economy resulted in a reduction in tax revenues to the state, thus requiring Alpha State University to reduce its budget. Although private institutions are generally not influenced directly by a reduction in state revenues, an economic downturn impedes a student's ability to pay, thus increasing students' financial needs and increasing the amount of institutional financial aid needed. Indirectly, state budget problems may also influence financial aid programs for students who attend private colleges and universities. Both scenarios usually result in increased tuition rates to replace lost revenue. An economic downturn also threatens endowment earnings, annual giving, and state and federal spending on grants and contracts. During economic boom times, both public and private institutions tend to share the wealth because state and federal agencies have more funding available, endowments and their earnings grow, annual gifts from alumni and friends increase, and philanthropy from business and industry and private foundations is high.

Differences. Private and public institutions nevertheless have characteristics that result in differences between them with respect to financial issues.

Institutional Governance. Governance marks one of the central distinctions between private and public colleges and universities. Private institutions tend to have large boards that are self-selected by the current board. Criteria for appointment may be influenced by affiliation; for example, an institution affiliated with a particular religion may have a religious requirement for membership on the board. Most private governing boards have categories of membership, and most include representation from graduates, major donors, and the business and legal communities, and most strive for women and minority representation. Also, some require a minimum donation for membership.

Boards in public institutions tend to be smaller, and members may be political appointees or may be elected to serve. States vary in how appointments are made, and they usually are determined by state statute. The selection process may consider a combination of legislative district representation, governor appointees, political office function, legislative approval, and election. State institutions have no formal role in the selection process and may influence membership only through their government liaison office.

The boards of public institutions may face considerable political and public pressures, whereas pressures on the boards of private institutions tend to be more internally focused and respond to the needs of such stakeholders as graduates, students, parents, and faculty.

State Funding. "Funds from the state government are the primary source of income for most public colleges and universities" (Barr, 2002, p.13). A reduction in state funding can have a large impact on the university's budget, as illustrated in the case of Alpha State University. State funding is not a factor or is a minimal factor in providing resources to private institutions. Although not a significant factor for private colleges, most receive state revenues from state-funded scholarships and other financial aid programs for residents attending private schools (Schuh, 2000).

Flexibility. Flexibility in the use of money can differ in public and private institutions. The budgets in private institutions are controlled completely by the governing boards. They determine the total operating budget, the sources of funds, and allocations. In most states, higher education funding is formula-based, while in others, legislative review of institutional budgets is extensive, potentially involving the screening of each budget line. State budget decisions tend to be influenced by the legislature and state governing boards.

Independence. The ability to determine an institution's options differs somewhat in public and private institutions. The leadership of a private institution needs only be concerned about and plan for a single institution, whereas a state may have several colleges and universities that need to be considered in planning and funding. Except in rare instances, state institutions are part of a state system of higher education. In these cases, the state legislature usually passes one higher education budget and the governing boards make the decisions on institutional budgets.

Final Budget Approval. In both private and public colleges and universities, the respective governing boards grant final budget approval. In private institutions, projected enrollment is the main contingency in final approval of the budget. A budget may be passed as presented, but if the actual enrollment is less than what was budgeted, the budget must be revised because there is less tuition income. Some private institutions wait until the fall board meeting to determine salary increases in order to ensure that the income projection is accurate.

Although enrollment figures tend, as in the case of Alpha State University, to be part of the funding formula in public institutions, in most states, any tuition revenue due to enrollment increases beyond the formula accrues to the institution. Also, the health of the state budget may have an even greater impact in a given year. If state revenues decline during the year, the legislature has the authority to mandate midyear reductions.

Given the similarities and differences in the climate of public accountability, higher education, whether private or public, is scrutinized by government, accrediting agencies, watchdog groups, parents, and students. Each stakeholder group wants assurances that resources are allocated appropriately, that productivity is high, that standard accounting procedures are used, that correct policies and procedures are in place, and that ethical leadership exists. As institutions undertake the budgeting process, it is important that the process be transparent, that the decisions be defensible, and that the leadership be accountable.

Conclusions and Implications for Student Affairs

Whether the institution is public or private, the issues it confronts in financing student affairs are similar. Budget development is a shared institutional responsibility. Student affairs professionals share budgeting responsibilities and challenges with professionals in other areas of the institution, and it is a rare year when any division obtains all the funding that is sought. Being effective in obtaining a fair share of the funding available is an ongoing process of developing credibility in requesting and managing funds. To develop that credibility, budget managers in student affairs have the responsibility to carefully consider the allocation and use of funds in their areas.

The budget should be mission-driven. Student affairs should have or develop a mission statement for the division that complements the institution's mission statement. Being able to articulate what student affairs strives to accomplish in the context of the institutional mission is a first step in having others understand the importance and relevance of budget proposals.

Planning is an essential component to budget decision making. Many colleges and universities are now involved in institutional planning and use the priorities established as a guideline for budgetary decisions. Regardless of whether the institution has a planning process and a set of priorities, student affairs should develop a plan based on the institution's mission, the student affairs mission, and the division's vision or goals. That process makes it possible for all staff in student affairs to understand and support the purpose of the division within the institution.

Having an institutional perspective, as well as a student affairs perspective, is critical for collegial decision making. Financial credibility requires that those from student affairs who are involved in developing the institution's budget develop an understanding of and appreciation for the roles and challenges of other divisions within the institution. This helps the budgetary process be one of "us" rather than that of "we" and "they."

Understanding the fiscal environment is important. Timing is an important factor in budgeting, as illustrated in the two case studies. The planning year described for John Dewey College and for Alpha State University would not have been one to propose a costly new program that had not been previously discussed and that was not a part of the institutional or divisional planning process.

The most important part is working together. Institutional financial decisions should not be a competition but rather a collaborative process of professionals working together to make the best decisions for the students and for the institution.

References

Barr, M. J. "The Importance of the Institutional Mission." In M. J. Barr, M. K. Desler, and Associates, *The Handbook of Student Affairs Administration.* (2nd ed.) San Francisco: Jossey-Bass, 2000.

Barr, M. J. *Budgets and Financial Management.* San Francisco: Jossey-Bass, 2002.

Heller, D. E. "Student Price Response in Higher Education: An Update to Leslie and Brinkman." *Journal of Higher Education,* 1997, *68*, 624–659.

Institute for Higher Education Policy. *The Tuition Puzzle: Putting the Pieces Together.* Washington, D.C.: Institute for Higher Education Policy, 1999.

Schuh, J. H. "Fiscal Pressures on Higher Education and Student Affairs." In M. J. Barr, M. K. Desler, and Associates, *The Handbook of Student Affairs Administration.* (2nd ed.) San Francisco: Jossey-Bass, 2000.

Upcraft, M. L. "Affordability: Responding to the Rising Cost of Higher Education." In C. S. Johnson and H. E. Cheatham (eds.), *Higher Education Trends for the Next Century: A Research Agenda for Student Success.* Washington, D.C.: American College Personnel Association, 1999.

Woodard, D. B., Jr. "Finance and Budgeting." In R. B. Winston Jr. and others, *The Professional Student Affairs Administrator.* Bristol, Pa.: Taylor & Francis, 2001.

JOAN M. CLAAR, *before she retired, was vice president for student affairs at Cornell College in Mount Vernon, Iowa, and dean of students at DePauw University in Greencastle, Indiana.*

HAZEL J. SCOTT *is vice president for student services at Georgia State University in Atlanta. Previously, she was vice president for student services at Occidental College in Los Angeles.*

3

Although they vary a great deal in size and scope, student unions and activity programs share several financial constraints and challenges.

Contemporary Financial Issues in Student Unions and Campus Activities

Tim Schroer, Christana J. Johnson

Financial constraints have affected almost every aspect of higher education. Expenses have gone up; revenue has often not kept pace, leaving college and university departments struggling each year as to how to best deal with this constant challenge; and student unions and activities are not exempt from these issues. The problem is not likely to go away anytime soon and in fact may only get worse.

Each of the colleges and universities in America is unique, and they work hard to differentiate themselves from one another. The college union, while often sharing common goals and philosophies, varies greatly from campus to campus in both facilities and program challenges. Every institution is confronted with unique funding issues based on a variety of circumstances such as geographical location, mission of the institution, and enrollment numbers. There are probably as many different funding issues for college unions and activities as there are institutions that host them.

The college union has changed and expanded since it was first conceived in 1812 at Oxford College. What began as a place for debate and refreshment has become, for many campuses, the social and cultural center for the entire campus community (Butts, 1971).

College unions today house a wide variety of activities and services, including dining, banking, travel agencies, student activities and governance, art studios and galleries, and bowling alleys. A large number of them, either through a union programming board or through a student activities office, program for a wide campus audience. Movie series, outdoor recreation trips, and speaker series are just a few of the many programs that take place in college unions, all costing more and more money that often comes out of shrinking budgets and limited resources.

In the past, membership dues funded several unions and their activities. Today, many derive a substantial portion of their operating budgets from combinations of resources. Besides monies allocated to them by the institution, many unions receive additional income from user fees, corporate sponsorships, and revenue from the auxiliary services that they house, such as food service and bookstores.

By contrast, student activities offices often do not benefit from the revenues of auxiliary services. This is especially true at small, private institutions. With such varied programming obligations, the staff members of a student activities office may find themselves stretched to the limit along with their financial resources. Many programs rely on student activity fees. Although this income is usually earmarked for student activities offices and their programs, implementing activity fees has not gone unchallenged.

Challenges for Unions

The contemporary college union faces a number of financing challenges. Foremost among these are facilities, revenues from auxiliary enterprises, and staffing.

Facilities. In student unions, the costs of the facilities themselves have been greatly affected by recent trends. The past few years have seen both an increase in new construction and an updating of current facilities. One major reason for this is to maintain an institution's either real or perceived competitive edge against rival institutions. While providing the campus with modern and updated facilities, the college or university will frequently find itself with a large debt load and an even bigger operating cost. For example, a $1 million renovation paid for through borrowing funds will increase the debt service by approximately $50,000 a year at current rates. An increase in revenue must follow in order to pay what is owed. Many times an institution will find itself unable to absorb the greater cost of operation. This can be felt most frequently at midsize public institutions. Competition for students at these institutions is often quite fierce, and the need to have attractive facilities is especially important. The alumni base at these schools is seldom as large as at the bigger state universities, resulting in a smaller pool to tap for outside funding.

Updating a union in order to comply with various state and federal building codes—for example, fire codes and the Americans with Disabilities Act—can add significantly to the total construction cost for the facility. This may limit the number of "bells and whistles" that could be included in the final building program. A greater expenditure on improved infrastructure versus activity space is a consideration that must be taken into account during the initial planning stages of any union renovation.

Each institution must deal with facility maintenance. The repair of broken objects, updating of equipment and technology, and replacement of furniture and other daily use items can cause the operating budget to outpace both generated and fixed revenue. Technology upgrades are a must if the union is to be the center of the campus community. It needs to be wired and technologically up-to-date, and this only adds to the financial burden.

Auxiliary Revenues. Auxiliary services have been present in college unions for some time. These range from the college bookstore and food service operations to travel agencies, banking services, and vending machines. The range and extent of these vary from campus to campus; however, the college union is often the place to find these services on most campuses. Many of these services generate a great deal of annual revenue. Depending on whether they are provided in-house or outsourced, the amount of actual income for the institution varies considerably. The proceeds from a good number of these retail and auxiliary functions are often designated to go directly back to the union to fund its operation and activities.

Sometimes the need to generate revenue in order to maintain operation of the building has a negative effect on the programming of activities. Programming monies are rarely viewed as fixed costs but more often as discretionary; thus they may end up as the first item to be reduced in budget-cutting activities. Programming space can also seem to be wasted space when not in use. If programming space is perceived that way, this perception can bring forward suggestions for other uses for that area, some of which are not always practical or cost-efficient.

Earmarking revenue from auxiliary enterprises has typically been the model for large university unions but not at small private schools. Auxiliary operations in the union at small private institutions are not commonly designated for the union's operating budget but rather are directed to the college's general budget and reappropriated according to the college's needs and priorities.

Retail activities at the union are often limited due to broader institutional constraints. Exclusive campuswide contracts for vending, beverages, and food service usually restrict the amount of outside retail that a union can provide, since duplication of revenue sources needs to be avoided.

Recent years have brought to the fore a variety of issues related to auxiliary income. One of the most basic reasons, yet one that has the most impact, is that revenues have declined at many institutions. Several factors have contributed to this trend. Increased competition has affected many auxiliary services and the amount of revenue they can generate. In addition to a multitude of off-campus vendors and merchants, the increased use of the Internet, or e-commerce, has affected the traditional mode of commercial activity. The amount of time students spend on the Internet is astounding: some 86 percent of all college students go online for a wide variety of purposes (Jones, 2002). The ability for students to do their banking, plan their travel, and even purchase their books and supplies online has reduced money coming directly into college union auxiliary units.

To counter this decrease, many institutions have sought to increase their own forays into the world of e-commerce, and the college union is one area that could benefit from such ventures (Conway and Henry, 2000). Although much campus-based e-commerce has involved primarily the sale of bookstore items, some schools have expanded into travel, banking, and other commercial areas. Students' increased use of and reliance on technology has made this an area to be explored by more institutions. One drawback, however, is that if it opts to launch into e-commerce, the school must carefully weigh the expense of buying costly software against developing it in-house. Either option will, of course, entail additional cost for the institution (Conway and Henry, 2000).

For many schools, it is not the decrease in actual income that has been the concern but rather the allocation of that income to other areas of the institution. Financial constraints on an institution will force it to look for additional funding sources from within.

Monetary reserves used to be held on to by the college union for future repairs, equipment, and technology updating. These reserves are now perceived at many institutions as fair game for the general budget and are reallocated to meet other institutional needs. In addition to union reserves, many institutions have increased the percentage of overhead charges that auxiliary units pay back to them, thus decreasing the resources available for unions and activities offices for building operational and programming budgets.

Staffing. The staffing of a union can be quite a challenge. The hours of the building will naturally be set by the campus community, but how does one determine what and how much can be done by student workers and what needs to be done by professional staff and custodians? Depending on what the institution's budget can allow, the number of full-time or part-time custodians employed to clean the union may not be sufficient for the needs of the building. It may seem natural to use student workers for light cleaning; however, students tend to resist doing any type of custodial work, regardless of how light the duties. Student workers may particularly object if the expectation of custodial duties is not made clear in the early part of the interviewing and hiring process.

Challenges for Student Activities

A variety of challenges exist for staff in the contemporary student union. Among these are mandatory student activity fees, the development of attractive programming, burnout among student leaders, and developing alternative sources of revenue.

Mandatory Student Activity Fees. In 1996, Scott Southworth and two other plaintiffs filed a lawsuit against the University of Wisconsin claiming the university's practice of allocating mandatory student activity fee monies to student organizations that did not represent their views violated their First Amendment rights (Center for Campus Free Speech, 2000). The case was eventually brought before the U.S. Supreme Court in 1999, and in March 2000, in an opinion written by Justice Anthony Kennedy, the Court ruled that "the University may determine that its mission is well served if students have the means to engage in dynamic discussions of philosophical, religious, scientific, social and political subjects in their extracurricular campus life outside the lecture hall" (Center for Campus Free Speech, 2000). The Court also stipulated that the decision-making process for allocating mandatory student activity fee monies must be viewpoint-neutral; however, the Court did not define what that entailed. Hence in November 2001, before the Seventh Circuit of U.S. Court of Appeal, the university again defended itself from Southworth's claims that it was violating his constitutional rights; this time Southworth had reversed his original claim and filed on the grounds that the university's allocation process was not viewpoint-neutral (Center for Individual Freedom, 2002). While supporting the university's mandatory activity fee, citing that "numerous limits on the student government's discretion for awarding funds" and a "comprehensive appeals process. . . . sufficiently limit the University's discretion so as to satisfy the requirements of the First Amendment," the Seventh Circuit Court also stated that "student fee systems at public universities are presumptively unconstitutional if they fail to limit decision-makers with viewpoint neutral funding standards and prompt impartial review." This ruling paved the way for institutions to be challenged continually on the basis of whether or not there are satisfactory limitations to define viewpoint neutrality.

Student Activities Programming. In addition to the possible litigation stemming from the mandatory student activity fee allocation process, a student activities office whose budget is derived solely from student activity monies can be challenged and limited in the types of programs, services, and events it can provide by fluctuations of the institution's enrollment. Indeed, the only dependable ways to increase the budget are to raise the amount of the activity fee each student pays or to increase enrollment; however, students and administration are often unwilling to do either, especially given the current economic environment. The consumer-driven nature of our society has taught our students to go for the best-quality education at the best possible price. Raising the student activity fee even a few dollars increases the total cost of attendance and thus has the potential to alienate students and their families as they consider the total cost of their education.

An additional restriction on the raising of student activities fees is that the activity fee is frequently only one of many item-specific fees that a college or university will impose on the student. Technology, library, recreation, and health services are other areas that are commonly funded by dedicated fees and add to a student's total bill. Union and student activities professionals compete with these and other areas for additional fee revenue. Institutions are reluctant to increase fees for too many services, and activities programming is often not perceived as being as important as areas with direct bearing on the institution's academic mission, such as technology.

In spite of this limitation, students have come to expect "big name" concerts, speakers, comedians, and so on, on their own campuses; however, they are hesitant to provide the financial means for contracting these events. Student activities staff members then find themselves in the comprehensive fee trap, saying that the activity fee included in tuition is all-encompassing but being forced to charge additional admission fees at many of these events.

Once the student activity program has its budget in place, activity planners often compete with other departments for space in the student union and on the campus master calendar. Just as financial resources are finite on campus, so are available dates for major speakers or entertainers and events. Frequently, student activities programs are pushed aside as events viewed as more significant to the academic goals of the institution are given higher priority for choice dates and venues.

Student Leader Burnout. As if funding were not enough of a challenge, the student leaders of an activities office can prove vexing for the professional office staff. Often the number and quality of student leaders coordinating the programming of the office are insufficient for the number of activities being sponsored. Professionals and student leaders alike lament the fact that the same few students are involved in the planning and execution of most, if not all, events organized through the office and through student groups.

In addition, the tendency for student activities offices to rely more and more on members of student governments and programming boards to do a wide variety of projects and tasks that may traditionally have been done by staff members can contribute greatly to student exhaustion. Students are already stretched in trying to reconcile academic and other cocurricular obligations in their schedules. On many campuses, students might not be adequately compensated financially for their work, since stipends and honorariums are often among the first things to be eliminated as an institution's overall budget is decreased. Whereas the hope is that receiving a stipend would not be the main motivation for students to be involved, often it is a key factor in their willingness to hold time-consuming positions, especially if they must maintain outside employment to help fund their education.

Alternative Funding Resources. "Given the accelerating costs of higher education and provision of quality services, combined with reductions in state and federal support for higher education, new resources must be found to maintain educational standards and growth" (Cunard and Freeman, 1991, pp. 27–28). Whereas corporations and foundations have monies allotted for "promotion and marketing, which can be money earmarked for project sponsorship for [a] union" (Drnek, 1993, p. 24), more and more frequently, institutions are turning to the corporate sector for sponsorships and foundation grants as sources of alternative funding (Cunard and Freeman, 1991; Drnek, 1993), making the competition for sponsorships and grants "extremely tight" (Drnek, 1993, p. 26).

The benefits of receiving such sponsorships and grants are obvious and include the ability to do construction, renovation, and programming previously out of reach due to budget constraints; however, the drawbacks may not be quite so apparent. The pursuit of corporate sponsorships and foundation grants must match the values and mission of the institution (Cunard and Freeman, 1991), and an institution must think realistically about what it can give in exchange (Drnek, 1993). The advancement or development office of the college or university must be involved in the process, especially if alumni are included as fundraisers in a campaign.

A possible drawback once a corporate sponsorship has been obtained is the potential for the relationship between the institution and the corporation to expand in order to offer additional programs. Frequently, such expanded relationships end up compelling institutions to provide services that are not in the best interest of the campus community (Cunard and Freeman, 1991). Cunard and Freeman (1991) offer a final warning: "the short-term gain of additional financial reward can never justify a compromise of our fundamental commitment to our students' best interest" (p. 28).

Conclusion

So where does the current environment leave college union and activities staff? One familiar suggestion is to work much more closely in partnership with other areas of the institution, especially the academic side. Union and activities professionals need to make the case for maintenance of funding. If monies for programming and activities always seem to be low on the priority list, these staff need to do a better job of making their case. Tying the activities and functions directly to the mission and goals of the institution and asking the tough question "How does this affect and enhance student learning?" can put the focus on the importance of union and activity funding.

Collaborating with other units of the institution is also important. It is vital to see this collaboration not only as a budget survival tool but also, even more important, as an opportunity to share what unions and activities contribute to the life of the institution with a greater college administrative audience. Certainly, collaboration should occur with other units in student affairs, but looking to other divisions is crucial. This suggestion is not intended to be construed as an attempt to obtain additional revenue internally, as that is unlikely to occur often. It should be regarded rather as a way to stretch current budgets through cosponsorships and combining resources.

Working closely with the development staff on campus is also crucial to continued funding. It may be possible to identify potential donors who are able to finance activities ranging from an endowed speaker series to building construction and renovation. This is probably more common at private institutions but should be explored, within appropriate guidelines, at larger public institutions as well.

Student government associations (SGAs) should not be forgotten when it comes to building coalitions with other divisions of an institution, for they can be resourceful allies. If the SGA is well funded, it may be willing to contribute significantly to the financing of building projects or major speakers or entertainers. If the SGA is not well funded, it can be an effective ally in making the case for additional monies or serving as a source of new and innovative ideas for fundraising.

A few budget-saving measures have been applied for some time but may need to be used and expanded even more in today's economic environment. The practice of working with other institutions through block program booking organizations such as the National Association of Campus Activities is just one approach whereby student activity staffs have generated additional programming on limited budgets. Working with other units within the institution and perhaps even the surrounding community on some programming such as a speaker or movie series may be another way to both stretch budgets and introduce programming to a broader audience.

References

Butts, P. *The College Union Idea*. Bloomington, Ind.: Association of College Unions International, 1971.

Center for Campus Free Speech. "The Southworth Supreme Court Case," 2000. [http://www.campusspeech.org/southworth.html].

Center for Individual Freedom. "Seventh Circuit Adds New Constitutional Requirement for Student Fees," 2002. [http://www.cfif.org/htdocs/legal_issues/legal_updates/first_amendment_cases/un_constitutional_fees.htm].

Conway, G. P., and Henry, W. "Research Reveals Scale of College Union E-Commerce." *Association of College Unions International Bulletin*, 2000, *68*(5), 8–11.

Cunard, M. R., and Freeman, M. "Corporate Sponsorship: How Far Do We Go? How Do We Get There?" Paper presented at the annual meeting of the Association of College Unions International, St. Louis, March 1991.

Drnek, J. "Funding Alternatives." *Association of College Unions International Bulletin*, 1993, *61*(1), 22–26.

Jones, S. "The Internet Goes to College: How Students Are Living in the Future with Today's Technology." 2002. [http://www.pewinternet.org/reports/toc.asp?Report=71].

TIM SCHROER *is associate dean of community life and diversity and director of Buntrock Commons at Saint Olaf College in Northfield, Minnesota.*

CHRISTANA J. JOHNSON *is assistant dean of students and director of intercultural life at Cornell College in Mount Vernon, Iowa.*

4

This chapter discusses the fundamentals of financing health and counseling centers and also identifies contemporary issues related to financing these two services.

Financing Health and Counseling Services

Richard P. Keeling, Dennis Heitzmann

Before considering the specific patterns through which colleges and universities fund health-related programs and services for students—and the ways in which those patterns are changing—it is important to underscore the simple but vital fact that these programs and services are supported by institutionally related funding. It is no small thing that across a wide variety of institutional types, colleges and universities in the United States—which are, after all, neither health care organizations nor mental health agencies—have elected to provide health and counseling services for students. They do so not because they want to be in the health care business—and especially in today's context of competition in health care, not because there is no alternative way for students to get basic services—but because providing customized health-related services for students advances the mission of the institution and promotes student success. If by offering on-campus health and counseling programs colleges did not further important goals in education and student development, would those programs be justified? Why would universities re-create services available in the community—and in this case, services that are hard to administer and expensive to provide—unless providing those services somehow made it possible for them to do their work better?

Although institutions have used more or less similar funding methods to finance health and counseling centers, there are fundamental differences in the usual and customary patterns—and in the emerging variations—for those two related but structurally and functionally different kinds of agencies. Although we will note the common features, it is impossible to preserve clarity in regard to funding either health or counseling centers without discussing them separately.

NEW DIRECTIONS FOR STUDENT SERVICES, no. 103, Fall 2003 © Wiley Periodicals, Inc.

39

Historical Perspective: Health Services

Health centers preceded counseling centers in the programs and infrastructure of student services in higher education. The development of health centers responded to either clinical or public health needs; whereas many had, from their founding, a specific charge to care for students who were sick or injured, others arose when epidemics posed challenges in sanitation, disease control, and community health. In most cases, early health centers were funded through central institutional budgets. In the United States, college health centers arose before the invention of health insurance.

Many newly minted colleges, placed as they were on the pioneering edges of American society—or intentionally deposited in rural retreats, as a benign strategy to extricate students from the perverse influences of cities and reduce the density of available distractions—could not count on the existing local resources to provide adequate medical services for their students. Especially in the pre-Flexnerian era of unsystematized, unaccredited, poorly monitored medical education, it was not entirely unreasonable for a college to decide that the immediately available community practitioners were insufficiently skilled or even dangerous. (Today, though, the shoe has traveled to the other foot: many students—especially the ones who have never used the campus health center—regard college health services as second-rate operations that employ untrustable health care professionals with dubious qualifications to provide marginal care. The "real doctors" are across the street, in the community, or back home.) We are no longer pre-Flexnerian; multiple systems exist to promote or guarantee the quality of community-based health care, and the context has changed completely. The point is that colleges today do not have to provide medical care for their students; they choose to do so.

This choice represents a university's conviction that the same health care services that the citizens in their community—and their own faculty and staff—use are insufficient or unsuitable for their students. The issues are different today, but the impulse to make sure students can get appropriate medical care is preserved in the descendants of campus administrators of a century ago. Questions of access, range and scope of services, availability, patterns and formats of care, and cost are all important considerations as institutions of higher education decide whether to provide medical services. But central to all of them is the belief that health is deeply connected to learning and therefore cannot be left to chance.

Not only that: health as it relates to performance, student development, and academic achievement requires a specialized approach. The doctors in town may be good, skilled, and interested in students—but would students get lost in their practices? Would the seemingly low-intensity complaints of students get short shrift on a busy day—would they be deemed important enough to demand attention? Would the complex interweaving of mind and body, health and learning, adjustments and symptoms be appreciated in the symptom-centered world of our harrowingly efficient health care "system"? Would local health care practitioners of any discipline have—or make—the time to infuse prevention through clinical visits? Would health care delivered in the community by practitioners whose service population was a typical mix of ages and needs have the same focus on student development that colleges expect of their own health centers?

Historical Perspective: Counseling Services

Counseling, as a function, role, or service preceded counseling centers on American campuses. Prior to the emergence of the campus mental health specialist and the dedicated service unit, various university officials, physicians in the health center, deans, and advisers provided guidance to students who needed assistance in their personal lives. After World War II, counseling services emerged as entities, providing primarily vocational and educational counseling, with a limited degree of personal counseling. The 1960s and 1970s witnessed a striking proliferation of campus-based counseling centers and an associated expansion of personal and psychological services that matched the increasingly identifiable—and increasingly complex—psychological needs of students.

Current Context

The choice to provide specific health and counseling programs is not trivial; it represents one of the conclusions reached in an institution's assessment of what helps students succeed. It is only because of the convictions and priorities suggested by those conclusions that colleges and universities have funded health-related programs and services in the patterns we now recognize as usual and customary. That institutions have regarded those services as essential is proved by their decisions—ratified and sustained over many years—to require that funds be gathered in one way or another to provide health programs for all students and to locate the sources and management of those funds in the major revenue streams and budget processes of the college itself. In doing so, educational institutions differentiate health programs from many other optional services for which students individually contract or pay over-the-counter. In most cases, funding for health and counseling services is derived and implemented through methods that are themselves common to core institutional mission, priorities, and processes.

Today's health and counseling centers offer a broad spectrum of services to the campus community. In recent years, the same convictions that led to the development of institutional medical services in the first place have supported a far greater variety of health care service models and a broader spectrum of health programs. College health is no longer just college medicine; nurses, nurse practitioners, and physician assistants provide a large and growing proportion of the care students receive, and prevention programs—health promotion, health education, clinical preventive services, population and community health services, public health activities, and digital health programs—have become core elements of college health. In many cases, prevention programs share funding sources with the clinical operations of college health centers, but increasingly, they may be financed by alternative means, including grants and collaborations. These changes, however, have not shaken the basic commitments of colleges and universities to provide health care for their students.

Counseling centers—almost unknown fifty years ago—now offer individual and group psychotherapy; psychiatric services; vocational and career counseling; psychoeducational programming; consultation with student groups, faculty, and staff; employee assistance programs; psychological testing and assessment; environmental enhancement; research; training; and teaching. Indeed, what was cited as the exquisite value of the counseling center over two decades ago would appear to be even more true today: "not only has the concept of the counseling center received universal acceptance, but it would be difficult to cite an area of academia that has had more of a direct and lasting effect on a generation of students" (Schoenberg, 1978, p. xvii).

From a fiscal perspective, though, counseling centers may have become the victims of their own success. Concurrent with the growth and development of counseling centers have been burgeoning costs for the same, with budgets consisting primarily of staff salaries. While recognizing the potential value of expanding these services, budget administrators have nonetheless struggled with the search for an optimum cost-benefit ratio for counseling centers. In the worst of economic times, universities have been hard-pressed to consider the deconstruction or severe limitation of counseling services. Counseling center directors have been required to become increasingly creative and convincing in their efforts to claim their share of relatively fixed university funds in a soft economy.

For at least the past decade, respondents to the Annual Survey of Counseling Center Directors have defined the continuing and pervasive challenges facing counseling center directors and the administrators to whom they report. In a benchmark article on emerging administrative challenges for college and university counseling centers, Bishop (1995) outlined a variety of problem areas together with strategies for responding to them. Citing the directors' survey published by Gallagher (1992), Bishop noted that nearly half of the respondent institutions had experienced a reduction in the size of the counseling staff, with more than half indicating little or no annual increase in salaries, and over two-thirds losing funding in other budget categories. In the decade since then, the situation has continued to be challenging. In the 2002 survey (Gallagher, 2002), 65 percent of the respondents indicated "a growing demand for services with no increase in resources or fewer resources" (p. 5). At the same time, 83 percent of the centers reporting described continuing concern about the increase in numbers of more seriously disturbed students seeking services. As a result of these trends, counseling centers have been hard-pressed to maintain comprehensive services of high quality in a climate of fixed or declining budget dollars.

There is an indication that an increasing number of centers have stepped up their efforts to remain solvent by seeking new streams of revenue in the face of restrictive financial realities. For instance, according to the Gallagher survey (2002), whereas only 7 percent of the centers charged students for personal counseling in 1992, more than 15 percent assessed such charges a decade later. Moreover, 35 percent are now partly or fully supported by a mandatory student fee, compared to 26 percent in the earlier survey. Finally, 17 percent of the centers were taking "innovative action to earn income." The array of "innovative actions" reflects creative and nontraditional responses to budget restrictions—for example, contracting for licensing and certification exams, charges for extended therapy or specialized services such as psychiatric services, sale of self-help brochures, the pursuit of university development funds and donor activities, assigning a fee for workshop presentations, soft money grants, consultation services to intercollegiate athletics, police services, and human resource offices.

Major Patterns of Funding for Health and Counseling Programs and Services

We shall now review the typical ways in which health and counseling centers are financed. We discuss both standard features and emerging patterns of finance.

Standard Funding Methods for Health Services. The great majority of revenue supplied to support college health programs comes from two types of funding: institutional funding and student fees. Each will be discussed in detail.

Institutional Funding. Especially in smaller colleges, many liberal arts schools, and some moderate-sized state institutions, monies for the operation of health programs come from the college's general accounts. The source of funds in those accounts depends on the governance (public or private), wealth (endowment), and financial structure (proportion of revenue derived from tuition) of the institution. Across all of those variations, though, the common feature is that general institutional funds—collected, allocated, or apportioned to support the college's operations and programs—are used to pay the costs of providing health programs. This pattern of funding has become less common as a second option, student fees, has emerged as the preferred method of paying for health services. The fact that general institutional funds are, or have been, used to support health programs demonstrates, of course, a commitment to removing barriers to learning. In flush times, when the coffers of colleges are filled with cash, institutional funds may seem to guarantee security for health centers and the survival of their programs; conversely, in cycles of tight budgets, health centers, like other college operations, will suffer reductions in operating funds. But it is the use of student fees, rather than institutional funds, that has ameliorated the impact of the funding stress that has often been felt more acutely in counseling centers.

Student Fees. In many small and liberal arts colleges and in the great majority of state institutions of moderate or large size, fees collected from students form the primary source of revenue to support health-related programs and services. A substantial minority of counseling centers also now receive student fee support. Fee-based health centers are ordinarily auxiliary enterprises that are expected to match revenues with expenditures on an annual basis.

These fees may or may not be specifically and separately identified on a list of the institution's charges and on bills sent to students and their families. At one end of the spectrum, there is no specific acknowledgment of the "health fee" or announcement of its amount as a separate item in budgets or bills—but in the construction of the "term bill," an amount that functions as a health fee is built into the calculations. Institutions that use this model may or may not think of the revenue required to operate health programs as being collected through a fee; it is simply part of what students have to pay to attend school, but it is accounted for separately from ordinary tuition. At the other end of the spectrum, many larger public universities—especially in states with populist traditions—very clearly and specifically identify a designated, or "segregated," component of fees collected from students as the health fee, and the sole use of the revenue produced by that fee is to support health programs.

Funding health programs through fees is a matter of governance as much as financing; students often have a voice in the setting and changing (especially, the raising) of fees, including health fees, whereas they have far less influence on the level of tuition. There is, once again, a spectrum of degrees of separation between student governance and the fees student pay for health programs, from distant relationships in which students may periodically demand a voice but there is no consistent or sustainable administrative structure through which students contribute meaningfully to determining fees to tight arrangements characterized by very high levels of student involvement in fee setting (and, in parallel, often by similarly high levels of student participation in the governance of health programs). In a few institutions, in fact, students, through their elected government, have full oversight authority for the campus health program, including control of the health center's budget. Still common to all of these varieties of fee funding is an institutional idea that health is central to academic purposes and that it cannot be left to individual chance.

Students' willingness to tax themselves through the imposition of fees and to raise those taxes periodically cannot be assumed or predicted, especially when the total cost of going to college is perceived to be painfully high or when universities or state systems seem to be shifting the burden of paying for education more and more toward students and their families. Students may react negatively to fee increases that seem unconnected to improvements in services; if they view a health center as inefficient or unhelpful, they may freeze fee levels or, in rare cases, reduce them. Most universities, though, have policies in place to prevent the sudden or capricious undoing of health center budgets by angry or disaffected fee committees.

Alternative, Secondary, and Emerging Funding Sources for College Health Services. Other funding structures may supplement either of these basic models and even, in some cases, provide the bulk of the funds for operation of health programs.

Fee-for-Service Collections. Health care is often expensive, and some components of it—especially ancillary services, such as clinical laboratory tests, physical therapy services, X-rays, or prescription pharmaceuticals—become out-of-pocket charges for campus health programs. For reasons that include cost control; delineating basic, required services available to all students from "extra" care that may only be needed by a few; and covering out-of-pocket charges, many college health programs have supplemented their basic funding model with incremental revenue linked to providing certain specific services, equipment, or products. Doing so tends to reduce the per-student cost of providing health programs for most students by isolating and charging certain costs back to the students who incur them. The most common fee-for-service charges include the following.

Clinical laboratory tests. Some college health centers operate on-site clinical laboratories that perform tests of mostly low or moderate complexity. More difficult and less frequently performed tests are generally referred to local or distant laboratories operated by hospitals or freestanding laboratory corporations. Some colleges assess no additional charge to students for tests that can be performed in their own health center laboratory but do charge students (usually at cost) for tests performed elsewhere (in which case the health center has to pay for the test out of pocket). In recent years, however, it has become increasingly common for health centers to charge students some amount for any laboratory test performed, whether or not it is completed in the health center's own facilities. The amount charged may or may not cover the actual cost to the health center of performing the test.

Prescription drugs, over-the-counter medicines, and health-related consumer products. Pharmacy operations in college health centers range from modest dispensaries (which may consist of a few commonly used drugs—and never controlled substances—stored in a locked cabinet or supply closet) to comprehensive full-service pharmacies that rival chain drugstores in the scope and range of their offerings. As is the case with laboratory tests, health centers may charge students for all drugs provided or only for certain less frequently prescribed or more expensive pharmaceuticals. College pharmacies may also offer students—sometimes at discounted prices—over-the-counter medications, self-care treatments, vitamins and supplements, and health-related consumer products, from contact lens solutions and lip lubricants to condoms and personal lubricants. Whereas a single dose of an analgesic may be given without charge as part of the health center's care and services, almost all universities that offer nonprescription items do so on a sales basis.

Medical supplies and equipment. Fee-for-service charges are also used to cover the cost of certain medical supplies (dressings, for example) provided to students or for equipment (such as crutches) lent but not returned. As is true of starter doses of over-the-counter medicines, an initial wound dressing is generally provided free of charge.

X-rays. Only a minority of health centers operate their own radiology facilities, and in all but a tiny number of campus health centers, only X-rays of bones, sinuses, the chest, and the abdomen are taken. These procedures are relatively low in cost, risk, and complexity compared to interventional radiology (such as arteriograms used to detect coronary disease), computerized axial tomography (CAT scans), and magnetic resonance imaging (MRI) scans. Health centers may provide simple in-house radiological tests without additional charge or may collect fee-for-service charges or copayments for X-rays.

Special clinical services and procedures. Health centers may provide limited surgical services, such as the suturing of lacerations and biopsies of skin lesions. They may also offer on a fee-for-service basis certain health care services not covered by their base funding—for example, routine physical examinations (for purposes such as employment or study abroad), consultation with specialists (usually dermatologists, gynecologists, orthopedic surgeons, and specialists in sports medicine), physical therapy treatments, acupuncture, and massage therapy. Almost always there are separate charges for all or part of these services—for supplies and equipment (such as the needle holders, suture material, and sterile dressings used to repair lacerations), for the time and expertise of a professional, and toward the cost of special equipment needed to provide the service (colposcopes, physical therapy equipment, or ultraviolet light boxes). The charges may represent the actual value of the service, product, or equipment provided or may be variably discounted.

Copies of medical records. Students often request copies of their medical records for future health care providers, insurance companies, other universities (in the case of transfer or graduate study), or certain programs, such as the Peace Corps. To cover the costs of providing those copies, health centers often assess a small processing fee; this fee also discourages trivial requests for copies.

Fees for clinical visits. Recently, a greater number of college health centers have begun charging students a fee for clinical visits. This fee, usually set at a very modest level (typically $10 or less, though different fees may be established for different clinical services, with higher prices for more extensive, time-consuming, or resource-demanding care), functions as a user charge that permits the health center to differentiate users from nonusers from a cost perspective while defraying some of its expenses. This procedure may keep the overall student health fee or institutional appropriation from rising as quickly as it otherwise might because users pay a disproportionate amount for the health center's services. These fees function much like required copayments for health insurance plans—and with some of the same effects: they may discourage trivial or low-intensity visits but may also serve as a barrier to access to care for impoverished students, students whose priorities are elsewhere, or students who decide to wait and get health services back home during breaks or intersessions. Universities that charge visit fees have therefore developed accommodations to permit students who cannot pay to receive services.

When collecting fee-for-service funds, health centers may take cash, accept credit cards, or bill charges to students' institutional accounts. Note that in any of these conditions, the health center has almost no collection risk—that is, unlike many other health care operations, college health centers can, by using a reliable backup billing structure in the form of the bursar's accounts, count on nearly 100 percent collections. This factor allows prospective budgeting for fee-for-service revenue with a high degree of accuracy.

Third-Party Reimbursements. Only a few years ago, very few college health centers collected revenue for the services they provided directly from insurance companies. This is an aberration in that almost every other health care system in the United States routinely bills insurance companies and collects payments from them to cover the cost of care provided to their covered subscribers. In fact, it is an aberration even in the context of students' lives; most of them depended on health insurance to pay for their health care before they came to college and will do the same after they graduate. They furthermore use health insurance to pay health care costs intercurrently with their college matriculation when they receive services back home or in the community.

Colleges and universities have historically not billed health insurance companies for a number of reasons—although they may have assisted students in preparing their claim forms when students sought reimbursement from insurance companies for fee-for-service charges made in the health center. Primarily, colleges have generally considered that services provided in the health center were already paid for either through appropriations from institutional funds or by payment of the student health fee. Charging health insurance companies for clinical visits thus seemed superfluous and unnecessary. Equally important, health center funding mechanisms, based as they are on general institutional monies or designated fees, were guaranteed (not at risk in relation to the quality of care provided, the number of students seen, or the rate of utilization of the health center) and predictable (based on known quantities, such as headcount or predetermined institutional budgets) and accounted for elsewhere (the health center simply received funds funneled from the bursar). The management of money in the health center was not complex. Health centers then did not usually want or need to have billing offices, substantial financial or business operations, or the expertise required to manage collections. Finally, health centers were committed to providing equal care to all students, regardless of financial or insurance status, and feared that billing insurance companies would set up barriers to access and establish different levels or grades of care. Many colleges feared that a large proportion of students were uninsured or underinsured (because of poor-quality insurance products—many of which, paradoxically, were sponsored by colleges themselves—or because of the rules of health maintenance organizations with tightly controlled access requirements and very limited provider networks).

More recently, though, the need for additional revenue to support operations and reduce dependence on student fees or institutional funds has made third-party reimbursements a more attractive option for campus health organizations. Health centers may bill students' insurance for ancillary services—laboratory tests, prescription drugs, X-rays, physical therapy, minor surgery—or for office visits to practitioners (or both). So far, many more health centers have chosen to bill insurance directly for ancillary care than have done so for office visits; the complexity of coding, billing, and collecting for office visits is far greater than that for standard ancillary services. By billing insurance for ancillary services, health centers can reduce or eliminate extra out-of-pocket charges to insured students while covering their own costs of ancillary care. It is necessary, however, to establish both infrastructure to conduct insurance billing and procedures to guarantee that uninsured students are not disadvantaged, without committing insurance fraud; billing only students with insurance would disadvantage insurance companies, discourage the purchase of insurance, and (most important) violate insurance regulations. Since laboratory tests, prescription drugs, X-rays, and other ancillary services are not difficult to bill to insurance—insurance companies simply establish payment levels for each item, and the health center files claims for the number of those service items delivered—the barriers to third-party reimbursement for ancillary care have been relatively few, and the practice has spread quickly throughout the field.

Barriers to billing insurance companies for office visits to practitioners are much more substantial. Office visits are simply not countable items of defined reimbursement value. The value of each visit must be established through standardized procedures (coding) that account, in an exceedingly complex way, for a wide variety of factors, from the length of the visit and the number of questions asked of the patient to the intensity of risk inherent in the medical problem and the degree of complexity involved in sorting that problem out and making treatment decisions. The codes assigned to visits, diagnoses, and procedures done establish the level of reimbursement allowed by insurance companies—and unsurprisingly, insurance companies are eager to avoid paying for more services than were actually provided or for services that they deem unnecessary. So it is that claims submitted by health care organizations of any kind—not just college health centers—are subjected to a rigorous review process; insurance companies commonly (indeed, routinely) question claims, refuse payment, or require additional documentation. Since insurance companies are eager to minimize payments and health care organizations are intent on being paid for the services they believe they provided, there is an inescapable tension—and often open conflict—between the two. Coding, documentation, the adjudication of claims, audits, and the process of resolving disputes are time-consuming, intense processes associated with high rates of staff turnover and job dissatisfaction. The record-keeping and information-processing requirements of successful insurance billing for office visits are high. Health care organizations that seek third-party reimbursements without installing substantial infrastructure and staff to support that effort are doomed to low rates of collection.

Relatively few college health centers have had the resources or the expertise required to conduct full-scale insurance billing, and viewing student fees or institutional appropriations as adequate payment for clinical visits, they have not had the motivation to make third-party reimbursements work. But when state or university funding is reduced, budgets are restricted, and ceilings are placed on increases in student fees, health centers entertain the possibility. Billing insurance companies does not require abandoning central funding or student fees. Those core funding sources can reasonably be regarded as the campus equivalent of taxes that support public health care facilities and hospitals; they guarantee access, pay for infrastructure, and in the case of college health, support the essential nonclinical services (health education, health promotion, outreach and wellness programs, demand management, academic liaison services) that are not reimbursable by insurance companies. Third-party reimbursements cover the costs of providing reimbursable clinical services—office visits and ancillary care—but not the basic operational costs of the health center.

Billing insurance companies generally also means charging students a copayment for services—especially in the case of office visits. While this is a usual and customary procedure in our health care system—and will therefore not seem unusual to most students—it represents a material change in procedure for many health centers. Whether third-party reimbursements are used to pay for ancillary services, office visits, or both, health centers that bill health insurance companies also need to establish policies, procedures, and mechanisms to provide the same care to students who do not have insurance and for students who are medically indigent—some of whom cannot pay the required copayment. Most health centers accommodate uninsured students by billing everybody for services, accepting assignment of payment from students' insurance companies, and writing off any charges not reimbursed by the insurance company that the student cannot pay (this is known as a "zero-balance write-off policy"). Students who meet the test of medical indigence receive care without payment of charges in accordance with established, fair policies.

Grants and Contracts. College health programs have sometimes obtained competitive grant funds to support certain services—especially prevention programs.

Alcohol abuse prevention. Several foundations (in recent years, notably, the Robert Wood Johnson Foundation), state agencies (especially alcoholic beverage control boards and traffic safety agencies), and federal programs (famously, the Department of Education's Fund for the Improvement of Post-Secondary Education, or FIPSE) have provided grant funds to institutions of higher education to support research or intervention projects designed to reduce alcohol consumption, control underage drinking, or ameliorate the harm done by high-risk drinking on campuses. Health centers are sometimes—but by no means always—the institutional recipients of these funds. Either in-kind or cash funding matches are often required. Programs funded by grants are subject to discontinuation, of course, when the "soft money" runs out. Attempts to institutionalize alcohol prevention programs during the period of funding, in an attempt to prevent the loss of good services when external funding ends, have been only marginally successful. Whereas foundation and government grants cause little controversy, alcohol prevention activities funded with the support of the alcohol beverage industry have caused strong differences of opinion. Can an industry-funded initiative truly reduce alcohol consumption—even if the industry claims to have no control over the programs developed with its funds? Despite hard times in prevention funding, relatively few health programs have chosen to seek or accept industry-funded grants, most of which currently support social norms interventions.

Disease prevention. The federal Centers for Disease Control and Prevention (CDC) have provided limited funds to higher education organizations, coalitions of colleges and universities, and occasionally to individual institutions to implement disease prevention programs, especially for sexually transmitted infections (notably, HIV/AIDS).

Violence against women. The Department of Justice recently funded two-year demonstration projects designed to prevent sexual assault and other violence against women and to improve services available to survivors.

Research Awards. Some larger and more comprehensive campus health centers may participate in research projects funded by the makers of prescription drugs, vaccines, or laboratory tests. These research awards may provide low-cost or no-cost services for students who agree to participate as research subjects. They rarely, if ever, contribute in any substantial way to defraying the costs of health care or operations for health centers.

Discretionary Funds. Essential prevention programs, especially, may be started, temporarily funded, revived, or restructured using discretionary funds provided through university administration, the alumni association, the nonalumni parents fund, or a campus-community task force. These funds virtually never support ongoing services.

Outsourcing. Colleges may believe that their costs in providing health care can be reduced by outsourcing the operations and management of campus health centers to private vendors (similar to outsourcing college bookstores, food services, physical plant maintenance, sports marketing, residence halls, or convenience stores). While this option may in fact reduce institutional costs, it may do so at the expense of important clinical or prevention services—although contractual arrangements may protect an institution against certain negative outcomes. The most successful outsourcing arrangements seem to occur when a local or regional hospital or health care organization provides the on-campus service; there are a number of examples of such contracts that are reported to work well for students and the institution.

Outsourcing not of the health center itself but of specific health-related services—especially ancillary care—is, by contrast, very common. Many health centers use local or regional hospital or corporate reference laboratories to provide in-house or referral clinical laboratory services. Several vendors of dispensary systems assist college health centers in providing safe, secure drug dispensing. Few health centers develop their own management information technology; most purchase systems from vendors. Health centers that wish to collect reimbursements from insurance companies can use the services of vendors to support and facilitate that process.

Retail Sales. A distinct minority of campus health centers derive a revenue stream from merchandising certain products—not including over-the-counter drugs or other health-related consumer items, which are provided on a fee-for-service basis—to students or others. Most often the products available for sale are somehow related to health promotion and outreach efforts under way at the institution. The health center may sell, for example, T-shirts or caps emblazoned with the center's logo or some health education message. Since few health centers have the expertise or infrastructure to conduct sales activities effectively—and since the cost of sales tends to be high—the contribution made by retail revenue to a health center's budget is usually trivial.

Counseling Centers

In this section, we will explore traditional patterns of funding for counseling centers and, thereafter, emerging and novel ways of financing counseling centers.

Traditional Funding Patterns. The traditional counseling center has operated under a simple budget process: a range of services are defined, operating costs are set, and the administration carves out a dollar amount from general institutional funds believed to adequately support the service.

Range of Services and Service Limits. Counseling centers continue to face a dilemma. To justify their importance (and at worst, their existence), a center's activities and programs must be comprehensive in the sense that they serve an increasingly large number of students. Criticism of purely clinical service was addressed early on by Drum and Figler (1973), who wrote, "Counseling services cannot demonstrate that they are helping a significant portion of the student body despite the fact that they have waiting lists. . . . Administrators are unimpressed because counselors are still talking about a small fraction of the student body. . . . Educational administrators are requiring counseling services to demonstrate that they are relevant to the larger portion of the student body and that they operate in the mainstream of the educational institution" (p. 74).

That clarion call from thirty years ago remains true today, perhaps to an even greater degree. As a result, counseling centers are remiss if they do not convey to the campus community that their importance goes beyond the mere provision of clinical services. Whereas the latter remain the cornerstone of counseling center activity, the wise administrator rallies the staff to provide a broader range of services that enmesh the center's activities in the fabric of the institution. The dilemma, of course, is that broadening services increases cost. There is no question that since the 1970s, counseling services on most college campuses have endorsed the strategic plan for selective but broad-based and comprehensive services. Even in an era of increasingly challenging student clients and reemphasis on clinical services, counseling centers have not lost their enthusiasm or their interest in providing the broader range of services to the campus community. To provide available staff time and to avoid cost overruns in the absence of significant budget increases, most centers have endorsed short-term therapy, whether through formally established session limits or by an intentionality to limit clinical services' duration to only what is absolutely necessary. In addition, the development of group therapy and referral to the community for long-term cases has allowed counseling centers to operate within their budget while serving the preponderance of students.

Institutional Funds. The early and for many campuses enduring mode of financial support for counseling centers came in the form of institutional funds' being designated explicitly for that purpose. Simply put, once established, the counseling center's budget remained essentially the same from year to year save for growth spurts or losses in institutional enrollment, the ebb and flow of the economy, the proliferation of special programs, and strategic plans for student affairs funding. As is true for health centers, the security in being embedded within the university's education and general budget is comforting in the best of financial times but places the center and its programs in jeopardy in the worst. During bad times, it is incumbent on the counseling center director to justify and demonstrate accountability for the range of services offered to the campus community. In a highly competitive financial environment where dollars tend to gravitate toward the "academic side" of the institution, some counseling centers may be bereft of the usual support. As a result, a number of alternative methods for funding have emerged that allow for flexibility and control, given the vagaries of institutional funding formulas.

Emerging Trends in the Funding of Counseling Centers. Several trends have emerged in the funding of counseling. We'll take a look at ten of them.

Fee-for-Service Revenue. One of the venerable values of counseling centers is not only to provide services but also to provide them at no cost to deserving students who have paid tuition to attend the university. This norm has eroded over the years, however, as some administrators have allowed for minimal charges to students on a fee-for-service basis. Following the lead of many university health services that have long charged for certain specialized services, counseling centers are becoming increasingly comfortable with the same idea. Typically this translates to a nominal fee for certain services and often takes the form of excess visit fees (for example, in a brief therapy framework, the fee "kicks in" after a certain number of sessions) or fees for specialized services (for example, psychiatric services, psychological or career assessments, and alcohol or other drug assessments and services). One of the pioneers in the expanded fee-for-service model was Milton Foreman, former director of the University of Cincinnati Counseling Center. More than two decades ago, his center was funded on a fee-for-service basis—including the collection of third-party payments. While establishing moderate fees for therapy, Foreman's counseling center ensured that mandatory insurance coverage for students endorsed mental health services as part of the contract. However, as Foreman noted, the danger in becoming an auxiliary enterprise is that the counseling center can be left "out on a limb" and viewed as self-sufficient by the institution, now limited to contracting with insurance carriers and selling the most cost-effective services to consumers as a way of generating the budget. This does not portend well for other vital activities of the center, such as consultation and outreach programming, which could be compromised by a clinical revenue model. Be that as it may, third-party insurance billing and reimbursements are likely considerations, particularly in tight financial times.

Mandatory Student Fees. Of the 274 institutions reporting on the Gallagher survey (2002), 41 (15.1 percent) indicated that they are supported fully by a mandatory fee, and 54 (19.9 percent) indicated partial funding through such a fee. This represents a gradual but continuing trend—already well established in health centers—in the direction of assessing surcharges for restricted health-related services. In this model, the onus for funding shifts from the university's education and general budget to an assessment attached to the students' fees for tuition. Typically, on an annual basis, a panel consisting of students and administrators reviews the program efforts, the cost to continue the program or expand it, and its benefit to student consumers. While recognizing that not all students will avail themselves of counseling services, it is assumed that all students are eligible for services. Under this model, it is incumbent on counseling center directors to tailor their accountability efforts to the student body. On the one hand, there is an advantage in the fact that the center no longer competes with other student affairs units for limited dollars. On the other hand, detractors of this financing method note the vagaries of convincing a constituency that is marked by rapid turnover, capricious valuing of services, and a high expectation of accountability.

Grants and Contracts. Most institutions reserve funds for special projects, from innovative ideas to research to diversity initiatives. Moreover, national organizations, state and federal governments, and private funding sources offer additional opportunities for the complementary funding of counseling center activities. Every center should ensure that attention is being paid to this rich resource as a way of enhancing and expanding current center offerings. A limitation, however, is that these funds typically come with strings attached. That is to say, there is an expectation that by the end of the grant, the center will have found some way to secure permanent funding or to absorb the program into the existing operation.

Contracting with On-Campus Units. Counseling centers would be remiss in not capitalizing on other forms of service to the campus community that may generate additional discretionary funds. Many counseling center staff, by virtue of their training and experience, have a broad range of services to offer the campus at large. For instance, process and organizational consultation with administrative and academic departments and the office of human resources, specialized services for athletes, employment screening assessments, and classroom instruction may generate funds that can ultimately be recycled in support of student counseling services. Since many of these needs would be contracted with community professionals (often at higher costs), a demonstrable savings without compromising quality would make the counseling center an attractive option. The assumption is that any funds generated for center staff would be retained by the center to be used at the discretion of the director.

Outsourcing. In the early 1990s, during a protracted economic downturn, great concern was expressed about the possibility of outsourcing counseling services as the most cost-effective way to provide counseling services to students. The threat was great enough that the Association for University and College Counseling Center Directors assembled a task force to look at managed care, outsourcing, and the implications. A think tank of twenty-two directors met at the Pennsylvania State University to discuss the growing concern about what appeared to be a cost-effective alternative to traditional funding for counseling centers. Ultimately, the task force concluded that the best defense against outside encroachment was for counseling centers to become the very best at what they do and to do so in a cost-effective manner. The managed care threat proved to be ill-founded, and the few institutions that experimented with this option eventually reverted to in-house service. Collegiate Health Care, Inc., the most ambitious purveyor of these services at the time, has since gone bankrupt and is no longer in business. In spite of the outcome of this episode, outsourcing may recover a role whenever the cost-benefits index of counseling is called into question.

Ancillary Funding Sources. Relatively minor, but no less important, are opportunities for enhancing a budget such as offering licensing and certification exams, the sale of self-help brochures, the development and sale of videotaped workshops and Web-based courses, and the assignment of a fee for external consultation and workshop presentations. Charging fees for these and similar efforts allow the director to use discretion in assigning revenues to the areas of greatest need. Whereas this array of ancillary services does not provide for an operating budget in its entirety, the additional dollars generated can take the edge off budget restrictions and allow for program initiatives that might not otherwise be offered.

Development and Fundraising. An underused opportunity for counseling centers lies with the development office. Although university development offices have historically ignored the needs of student affairs units in general and counseling centers in particular, development opportunities remain a vast untapped resource. Donors do exist, and counseling and mental health services have an emotional pull for many would-be donors. Donor support for specific programs, from suicide prevention to depression screening to capital projects, is realizable, given the thrust of a targeted development campaign. Indeed, centers that offer career counseling and placement services may be in a key position to garner corporate support in view of mutual interests in establishing high-quality placement services. At the very least, counseling centers need to become familiar with the development office and to lobby for a member of that unit to be assigned specifically to the counseling center or to a comprehensive student affairs effort.

Collaborative Partnerships or Consortia. Counseling centers open to collaboration would profit from consortia or partnerships with other institutions, resulting in enhanced services across all of the participating institutions. Based on the model of psychology internship consortia, regionally or locally based institutions can share costs and services that would yield an enhanced fiscal position for all. For instance, many of the larger university campuses have academically based training clinics in the doctoral programs as well as student counseling centers. Although the administration may tolerate these for training purposes, an opportunity exists to share both administrative and clinical costs, through collaborative planning and management. The economies of scale could result in savings to be used in support of their respective missions.

Funding Health and Counseling Programs in the Future: Challenges of Change

The funding approaches for health and counseling services used in the future will be different from the approaches used in the past. Here we outline some of the fundamental changes that will occur.

Health Centers. It seems unlikely that college health centers will be able to sustain their basic funding models without modifications in the future. Despite the undeniable value of health to learning, health care itself has become so commoditized in the United States that campus health centers are losing their claim to special protection through guaranteed funding streams. Students coming to college are more sophisticated health care consumers than their predecessors; they expect both convenience and efficiency, and they will shop—using their insurance plans—for providers who meet their needs and produce higher levels of satisfaction. It is less common today for students in college to define themselves purely, or even primarily, by their student status; just as their education happens across a porous boundary between campus and community and through digital and human networks that challenge a college's idea of control over curriculum, their health care may be obtained and paid for on or off campus, depending on circumstances, convenience, and preference. Accustomed to high consumer values in their precollege health care, many students are dismayed to discover a more limited array of services in college health centers. Pressure for more, better, and more easily accessible services will drive health centers to provide new kinds and levels of care—some of which will not seem immediately related to student development, learning goals, or institutional mission.

Although demands are increasing, resources are not infinitely elastic. Institutions that fund health centers directly from core funds likely will reevaluate the wisdom of that strategy as competition for limited funds increases. When money gets tight, will the college choose to support—or increase support for—a health center or preserve an academic department? State after state has restricted the growth of tuition and fee levels on the one hand while struggling with diminishing resources on the other. Health centers, facing more limited resources, will have to make harder decisions about priorities and programs. Direct clinical services will always win; there is, after all, a waiting room full of students needing care, and in many institutions, residence halls and off-campus housing areas function as incubators, preparing other students to enter the waiting room. Nonclinical services will almost inevitably be sacrificed or restricted when finances are under stress—despite the fact that the prevention programs of college health services are often more closely linked to academic and developmental outcomes than clinical activities are.

To prevent losing essential prevention programs, some health centers will turn to grants, contracts, discretionary funds, and research projects—but they will find the number of available programs, and the levels of funding offered, disappointingly low. Many will look for alternative sources of clinical revenue to protect their budgets against stabilization or reductions in core or fee funding. Fee-for-service revenue and third-party reimbursements will become increasingly common, and third-party reimbursements, initially limited mostly to payment for ancillary services, will likely expand quickly to include office visits. Financing in college health will likely become more complex, and managing money in health centers will demand more infrastructure and expertise than has been needed until now in most settings. Health centers will seek—and inevitably, the private sector will provide—flexible tools and services to support those activities. More and more, directors' time, efforts, and mind share will be focused on funding; revenue that might have seemed virtually risk-free and guaranteed at one time may look very different just a few years from now.

None of our projections are undesirable outcomes, really. An undesirable outcome would be the discontinuation of health care on a campus or so severe a restriction in services that a campus health program no longer could fulfill its promise to support learning, improve academic achievement, and contribute to student development. A new funding arrangement is not necessarily a bad arrangement—even if it is materially different from its predecessor. Effective college health directors in the future will be agile managers of funding streams, careful stewards of what institutional or fee-based funds they still have, and competent overseers of the increasingly complex business operations conducted in their centers.

Counseling Centers. Counseling center managers and the administrative officials to whom they report face a similarly vexing problem. Relying exclusively on a traditional budget model (depending on institutional general funds) requires that a center be prepared to ride out turbulent financial times, dealing with budget reductions and staff limits or cuts until the economic climate improves. Unfortunately, to rely exclusively on that plan is to remain locked in an endless cycle of up and down, ebb and flow. To remain viable, some centers are finding the need to consider short- or longer-term solutions to budget challenges. The obvious recommendation is to seek other opportunities for budget enhancement—using any of the methods and sources described in this chapter—not only to improve on existing budgets but also to provide stability during an unstable economic climate.

What has not been mentioned in outlining the various considerations for financing counseling centers is the integral role played by the counseling center director. Ultimately, the best tool at a center's disposal is the director's ability to be influential, assertive, opportunistic, and savvy in efforts to secure continuing support for the center. The director needs to be fully aware of the financial and political climate of the institution and to be ready to assert the importance of the center when seeking a reasonable share of university resources. The director needs to collaborate and team up with the administration's leaders, recognizing that in most instances, the vice president for student affairs and other ranking administrators also want what they want, which is what is best for students. Directors need to inspire trust and confidence while remaining team players in every sense; strident, plaintive approaches have never bought a center much in the long run. Ultimately, the director strives to keep the counseling center at the top of the list for those times when university budgets allow for enhanced departmental increases.

For counseling centers, adhering to the traditional form of funding has its merits, since it ensures that the institution is mindful of the integral value of the center. Be that as it may, several decades of experience now indicate that the trend is toward ever-increasing opportunities to enhance, if not replace, the institution's share of the budget by implementing reasonable ways of supplementing limited budget dollars. Clearly, the director needs to walk a thin line between becoming overly entrepreneurial, thereby reducing the incumbency of the administration to provide adequate support, and resisting the same, risking a continuing erosion of the center's budget. Being astute observers of the political and economic climate, directors must carefully and thoughtfully wade through difficult times without panic or reactivity but have the courage to step up and offer reasonable short-term or long-lasting alternatives while consistently making it clear that counseling services have been, and will remain, vital contributors to the lifeblood of the institution.

References

Bishop, J. B. "Emerging Administrative Strategies for College and University Counseling Centers." *Journal of Counseling and Development,* 1995, 74, 33–38.

Drum, D. J., and Figler, H. E. *Outreach in Counseling.* New York: Intext, 1973.

Gallagher, R. P. *National Survey of Counseling Center Directors.* Alexandria, Va.: International Association of Counseling Services, 1992.

Gallagher, R. P. *National Survey of Counseling Center Directors.* Alexandria, Va.: International Association of Counseling Services, 2002.

Schoenberg, B. M. *A Handbook and Guide for the College and University Counseling Center.* Westport, Conn.: Greenwood, 1978.

RICHARD P. KEELING is chairman and executive consultant for Richard P. Keeling & Associates, Inc., in New York City. He served as director of health services at the University of Virginia and the University of Wisconsin–Madison and is a past president of the American College Health Association.

DENNIS HEITZMANN is director of the Center for Counseling and Psychological Services and affiliate professor of psychology and counseling psychology at the Pennsylvania State University in University Park. He is past president of the Association for University and College Counseling Center Directors and the International Association of Counseling Services.

5

*This chapter presents contemporary financial issues in
student housing programs framed through the topical
areas of occupancy management, facilities, new
construction, residential life programs, technology, and
residential dining.*

Contemporary Issues in Student Housing Finance

Mary Ann Ryan

When examining the cost of attendance at institutions of higher education,
room and board represents approximately 50 percent (30 percent private
and 66 percent public) of the expenses that students and their parents face
(National Center for Education Statistics, 2002, pp. 359–360). The financial impact of living on campus is substantial for students and their families. Although generally, housing directors "have had limited control over
room and board rates" (Schuh and Shelley, 2001, p. 45), they can educate
and often influence a larger campus community on financial issues facing
housing programs.

In years past, utilities, renovation, fire safety, maintenance, and
employee benefits were issues on the student housing agenda. Today, those
issues remain, joined by new challenges in the student housing financial
environment. Terminology such as *bandwidth, resnet, wireless, online services, ADA compliance, indoor air quality, sprinkler fitters, design-bid-build,*
and *24/7* is now relatively common in the student housing vernacular.
Students have high expectations for up-to-date service delivery and facilities that provide value. Individuals responsible for student housing programs must offer students safe and fully functioning facilities with modern
amenities and programs, all at reasonable cost.

This chapter will provide an overview of major financial issues affecting student housing programs. First, I will discuss occupancy management and then the financial challenges related to both existing facilities
and new construction. Next, I will examine the evolution of residential
life programs and the associated cost implications before moving on to the

financial implications of technology in the residence environment. I will then confront residential dining issues and end by giving some attention to planning.

Occupancy Management

Occupancy, as it relates to revenue, generally drives the student housing budget. Demographics, the university's mission and direction, policies, and competition often influence occupancy. Decisions regarding the size of the freshmen class, mandatory residency, guaranteed housing, or graduate and international student enrollment are generally made outside of the student housing department.

According to the National Center for Education Statistics (2001), overall the number of high school graduates nationwide is projected to increase to 3.1 million by 2010–11. This represents an 11 percent increase over the number of graduates in 1998–99. In that same time frame, some states will see a decrease in the number of high school graduates ranging from 1 to 22 percent. Much of the decrease is predicted for parts of the Midwest and Northeast (pp. 53–54). For many campuses, the number of new high school graduates in the state directly affects enrollment and residence hall occupancy.

Because housing occupancy can fluctuate over time, depending on demand, housing capacity is usually flexible. Expressions such as "double as a single" or "expanded housing" describe adjustments to the capacity to meet housing demand and maximize revenue streams. Some colleges and universities lease hotel or alternate space temporarily to accommodate the initial demand for housing. Usually the per-night charge from the hotel will be higher than the traditional residence hall rate. In addition, transportation and dining arrangements could increase the cost of this form of temporary housing. In this situation, the student housing department weighs the financial advantage of increased residence hall occupancy throughout the academic year against the potential revenue loss of the temporary hotel stay. In some cases, even when charging the traditional residence hall rate to the student for the hotel stay, there can be an overall financial gain.

At times, housing capacity also adjusts to decreases in individual student occupancy. Conversion of traditional residence hall floors to graduate and nontraditional living options, office space, guest housing, or other uses provide a continual revenue stream to offset fixed costs such as debt or overhead.

Policies also affect the student housing financial environment. Whether it is new admissions standards or a new definition of full-time student status, campuswide decisions may affect occupancy. Mandatory residency policies have long existed as a consequence of the research on the advantages for first-year students living on campus (Pascarella, Terenzini, and Blimling, 1994) and to maintain an occupancy level that is sufficient to fund the debt and other fixed costs.

Implementing flexible and carefully crafted assignment processes is crucial to ensure a strong occupancy base. When possible, many programs establish room reapplication policies, giving preferential treatment to upper-class students to increase retention. In situations where a shortage of housing exists, restrictions are placed on the number of current residents allowed to return to live in student housing the following academic year. To further complicate student housing assignments, opportunities to study abroad are becoming more commonplace. In some cases, residents spend a semester away from campus, expecting to reclaim their room or apartment upon their return. Also, when an academic program's duration does not coincide with the academic year calendar dates, the management of housing assignments to ensure optimal occupancy can be compromised. Reserved spaces for special programs, an increasing amount of contact with parents and their lawyers, upgrades to assignment technology, waiting list management, and requests for special assignment exceptions all take considerable staff time away from the major assignment process.

Projecting future occupancy is important from a financial standpoint. From a traditional student housing perspective, a surge in enrollment or new emphasis on the first-year experience may cause some members of the campus community to call for more housing on campus without first assessing the long-term demand. Conversely, a plunge in enrollment, empty floors or residence halls, or an overall shortage of campus office space could cause some members of the campus community to advocate for premature conversion of residence halls from student housing to other uses. Occupancy projections require an understanding of college or university strategic directions, demographics, past trends in enrollment and occupancy, and the off-campus market.

The position of the off-campus housing market as either a threat or an ally to the student housing department generally depends on housing demand in the area. From the mid to late 1990s, for example, the vacancy rate in the Twin Cities housing market was notably low, less than 2 percent in the area surrounding the University of Minnesota's Minneapolis campus. With a shortage of housing in the area and a rising freshmen enrollment, the campus welcomed developers who built quality housing that was reasonably priced for students.

Current Facilities: Issues and Financial Implications

Many traditional residence halls were built in the 1950s and 1960s after Congress passed Title IV of the Housing Act of 1950. The Housing for Educational Institutions program offered colleges and universities loans with low interest rates and long amortization periods for the repair of existing facilities and the construction of new housing (Frederiksen, 1993). As many campus housing facilities turn forty, fifty, or even older, a significant portion of student housing budgets is earmarked for repair, maintenance,

and preventive maintenance while administrators consider renovation, rehabilitation, and new construction. To do nothing in response to aging facilities became untenable in the 1990s (Stoner, 2000).

According to Stoner and Grimm (1996), a renovation should add more
than ten years to the life of the building and cost less than 70 percent of the
cost of new construction. Rehabilitation adds more than twenty years to
the life of the building and costs less than 80 percent of a new building.

Along with modernizing aging facilities and addressing deferred maintenance issues, changing federal and state laws and codes can require significant facility upgrades. Title II of the 1990 Americans with Disabilities
Act (ADA) requires that university programs, services, and activities be
accessible. New construction occupied after January 1993 must be accessible. ADA compliance has significantly increased renovation and new construction costs. For example, requirements regarding elevators, bathroom
size, equipment, and fixtures add to project costs and in some cases long-
term maintenance costs (Brice, Kallmyer, and Mielke, 1994).

The United States Fire Administration (2002) reports that there is a
new level of awareness regarding student housing fire safety as a result of
tragic fires on university campuses. When listing components of a safe residential living environment, Cowell and Gallagher (1998) note that sprinkler systems were the preferred means of automatic fire suppression. Some
campuses are retrofitting their residence halls with sprinkler systems.
Sprinkler installation, costing literally millions of dollars for most housing
programs with multiple facilities, was likely not in most capital plans ten
years ago.

It is no longer uncommon to hear about school or facility closings due
to toxic mold. Toxic mold is a facilities challenge with serious health, safety,
and financial implications. According to Weise (2001b), moisture is a cat-
alyst for toxic mold; therefore, proper restoration of water damage is essential to ensure residents' health and to prevent structural damage. Mold
removal, like asbestos abatement, can be costly. Relocating occupants while
addressing the mold problem results in revenue loss.

Mold, along with other bacterial contaminants, can pollute the indoor
air quality (IAQ); that presents another health risk for students and staff.
Monitoring the IAQ through coordinating maintenance activities in the hall
(for example, stripping floors, painting, exterminating), establishing responsible policies related to smoking and in-room cooking, and following a
proper maintenance schedule for the HVAC system can protect student
health and save money (Weise, 2001a).

Furniture made from particleboard can also have an effect on IAQ
(Weise, 2001a). Furniture decisions made today can haunt housing professionals for years to come. Dressers, desks, and even bolsters were built
into student room walls that now might be covered with noise reduction
materials such as carpet. When selecting furniture for student housing,
function, style, and comfort must be balanced against available space, cost,

and durability. Attention to ergonomics, placement of cords and cables affixed to electronic equipment, and overall furniture flexibility will serve the program well.

If adequate furnishings are not provided, students will improvise, possibly causing liability or storage challenges. The evolution of lofts in the residence halls is a prime example. To create additional floor space in residence hall rooms, students elevate their beds. Some campuses allow students to build lofts and in some cases provide guidelines and instruct the resident assistant to inspect the completed structure. Realizing the risk associated with this procedure, many colleges and universities provide loft kits that include guardrails and ladders. Providing appealing furnishings also reduces the need for storage of residence hall furniture. Storage space in residence halls is at a premium, given the conversion of floor closets to telecommunications and recycling rooms and the need to store expanded housing furniture.

Community bathrooms, traditionally shared by residence hall students, are trademarks of "dorm" living. Some colleges and universities upgrade this space with private showers, enclosed toilet areas, lockers, and in some instances audiovisual amenities. Eliminating urinals from restrooms refitted from exclusive use by men to exclusive use by women, making sink areas more private, and meeting current laws and codes all increase the expense of renovation.

Whether air-conditioning a summer conference hall or installing contemporary lighting in student rooms, the replacement or upgrade of new building systems is becoming more sophisticated and more expensive. Individuals responsible for student housing facilities need to be involved in the early planning stages of major projects and new construction to ensure appropriate feedback on building systems and equipment. Their input and involvement can reduce expensive repair and maintenance issues in the future.

Other facilities issues include floors, window treatments, and locking mechanisms. Facility access is moving from key to card to hand or eye recognition. This evolution is slow and costly; however, the advancements increase safety and security if properly managed.

Many of these facility issues apply to all student housing, including apartments. Compared to residence halls, apartments typically have lower density and may be prone to different issues due to the number of kitchens and bathrooms, design, era built, and style of construction. Issues such as playground equipment, on-site child care center, trash removal, and parking further complicate student housing facilities planning.

The inventory of many student housing programs does not include Greek housing located off campus. Fraternities and sororities, like traditional student housing programs, strive to create community in a cocurricular environment. When Greek housing occupancy declines and code deficiencies and deferred maintenance accumulate with no apparent solution, the institution needs to assess its obligations and liability. Although mandatory occupancy requirements are spelled out in some Greek letter organization bylaws, lack of enforcement or falling membership can present problems. Does the issue of Greek housing deficiencies belong to the student housing department? Although frequently complicated by ownership and location, these houses reflect on the college or university. Their future merits conversation and in some cases financial support.

Summer conference housing can bring additional revenue and serve as a recruiting opportunity for the college or university (Hallenback, 1993). Scheduling residence hall summer use is often influenced by capital projects and cleaning schedules as well as the client's desire for specific campus locations and air-conditioned or non-air-conditioned space. Summer conference rates can be complicated when considering youth and adult groups, sport camps, length of stay, frequency of room cleaning, linens, and meal requirements. Sometimes opening a dining hall just to serve a small group is not cost-effective but necessary for public relations or political reasons. Student housing departments attempt to set rates that cover operational and fixed costs and that seem reasonable to summer clients.

The needed improvements in current residence halls and apartments are often funded from reserves and, in the case of larger projects, through college or university debt. Some campuses fully fund depreciation and are positioned to implement timely repairs and renovations; however, some capital requirements or upgrades could not be foreseen years ago. In these cases, with a shorter financial planning time frame, rate surcharges or a reprioritization of capital projects are often necessary.

New Construction

When contemplating additional housing, many variables need to be considered. First and foremost, the college or university must know the long-term demand for student housing, who will be housed, and the number of beds needed. Determining how the housing will be built, what unit configuration best responds to student preferences, and what rents to use in the pro forma are important decisions made in the planning process. But ultimately, the financing of the new housing is the most critical component of the planning process.

Typically, colleges and universities consider debt capacity and bond rating when determining campus new construction priorities. When debt capacity is not available for new student housing or when the college or university decides not to issue bonds, other financing options are explored. According to Mielke and Jones (2002), some campuses have chosen to partner with private developers to design, construct, and finance new student housing. In some instances, the developer even offers off-balance-sheet financing and project management.

Terms and conditions of these partnerships vary from campus to campus. For example, the location of the housing (on or off campus), management arrangements, length of the agreement, and occupancy requirements (if any) are often unique to each campus. Lease arrangements or management agreements between the developer and the college or university are carefully negotiated. Some campuses treat public-private housing as part of their inventory for purposes of student application, assignment, and payment for the space and in some cases provide a residential life program in the facility. Other campuses keep the housing at arm's length in terms of all management functions.

Along with bonding and public-private partnerships, self-financing (borrowing money from the institution and repaying the loan with interest) and gift support are two other methods to finance a project (Barr, 2000).

The cost of new housing is predicated on a combination of decisions such as requirements in the program statement, site constraints, the choice to design-build or design-bid-build, selection of an architect, and college or university construction standards. Sometimes auxiliary student housing departments are expected to subsidize ancillary components of the project, such as new parking spaces or campus green space. Collaboration among all stakeholders is essential. Change orders (changes to the construction plans) during construction are costly and should be avoided.

Strong project management is necessary during the design, construction, and initial occupancy phases for the project to stay on budget. Timing is critical. If the construction is a new addition to an existing housing facility, the timing of the project could negatively influence current occupancy. Construction occurring in the winter months when the weather is cold can add to project costs. Finally, it is imperative that the new construction be ready for occupancy on time. Although the construction company may be penalized financially for late project delivery, from a public relations, logistical, and sometimes financial standpoint, a delayed opening is unacceptable to the students and the student housing department.

Residential Life Program

Financial issues in the residential life area include funding program expansion, increased specialization, and staff. Funding program expansion often includes capital improvements to existing facilities. The enhancement or creation of space that fosters participation or involvement supports active learning (Strange and Banning, 2001). Adding amenities enhances traditional residence hall programs. For example, daily newspapers, "free" laundry, a residence hall movie channel, and microwaves and refrigerators in each room are amenities that housing programs often fund through room rates.

As residential life programs have developed over the years, some program components have become more specialized, necessitating more staff or program support. For example, *Esteban v. Central Missouri State College* (1967) established due process requirements in great detail for colleges and universities (Kaplan and Lee, 1997). The administrative work associated with documenting the incident, issuing a statement of charges, scheduling a hearing, recording the findings, and sometimes even administering the appeal process can be overwhelming to coordinate systemwide and may require additional staff support. Cultivating and expanding living learning programs, administering the Ethernet program, enhancing housing market strategies through new publications and Web development, and an ever-increasing emphasis on student housing security may require significant financial support to implement properly.

At the 2002 Association of College and University Housing Officers—International annual conference, the shortage of residence hall director candidates was identified as a serious problem in the housing profession. The live-in nature of the position on most campuses causes housing administrators to examine hall director apartment conditions (number of bedrooms, availability of laundry, pet restrictions, furnishings, appliances, and access) and salary levels to help market the positions. Some institutions provide hall staff with the latest in technology as a means to market the positions. With competition for qualified residence hall director candidates increasing, financial resources are now in many cases dedicated to making the position more attractive.

Undergraduate positions for both hourly staff and resident assistants may also require additional funding. The number of hourly employees may increase as new programs or longer hours of operation for existing programs are implemented. The resident assistant position is receiving much attention lately. Some members of the profession are critical of the current resident assistant staffing pattern found on most campuses. Further, Palmer and Devine (2000) report that resident assistants are at greater than average risk of becoming victims of violence in the residence halls. The position has existed for decades with fundamentally the same job responsibilities and compensation plan. Annual rate increases to room and board (which usually constitutes some or all of the resident assistant's salary) are generally not viewed as raises by the undergraduate employee. In 2002, resident assistants at the University of Massachusetts, Amherst, voted to unionize (Schmidt, 2002). Undergraduate staffing patterns will continue to be discussed and in some cases dramatically altered in the years to come. The financial repercussions of potential changes are yet to be determined.

Technology

Typically, standard features of living on campus include high-speed data connections, access to hundreds of cable television channels, and telephone service with multiple options (Segawa, 1999). For the past two decades, service and program delivery, as well as marketing, has become increasingly

Web-based (Gore, 2000). Student housing programs have invested and will continue to invest considerable resources in technology. It is not enough to simply wire a residence hall for high-speed Internet access. Ongoing funding for support and upgrades is necessary.

Over the years, the evolution of telephone systems in housing facilities has affected student housing finances. For example, many programs experienced a loss of long-distance commissions as the availability of long-distance providers offering competitive rates increased. Student preferences for options such as voice mail, caller ID, and call waiting increase operational expenses. And with increasing numbers of students coming to campus with cellular telephones, the value of providing telephone service in each student room is being debated.

Housing Web sites are becoming increasingly sophisticated. Creating, testing, and rolling out the Web site and subsequently updating and maintaining a Web site are also relatively new expenses for student housing departments.

In many instances, students can apply for housing and make payment online using a credit card. The cost associated with accepting credit card payment, either online or through the mail, has a negative impact on the housing budget. Some students and their families choose to pay the entire bill for room, board, tuition, and fees with a credit card simply to take advantage of promotions offered by the card issuer.

More frequently, students are using wearable and mobile technology well suited to a wireless environment. Adapting student housing facilities to wireless technology will be a significant undertaking.

It is not uncommon for housing professionals to hear from the institutional technology professionals that residence hall students use a disproportionate amount of the campus bandwidth. In some cases, student housing programs are charged more for technology because some residents download excessive amounts of video and music.

Student housing must confront numerous decisions about the use of technology in the residence environment. Upgrading laundry rooms such that students can sit in their room and know if washers and dryers are in use or putting job orders, room inventory, and front-desk equipment checkout procedures online all provide convenient service to students. However, as Barr (2002) indicates, "there are many good reasons for installing technological innovations on a college campus. Saving money is not one of them" (p. 11).

Residential Dining

In some cases, residential dining is a component of student housing finances. When student housing and residential dining are considered one department, dining facilities are located in residence halls, and commissions from resident meal plan sales are part of the housing budget, the success of the dining program influences student housing finances. One could argue that even if housing and dining are not financially interdependent, when students participate in mandatory meal plans, their satisfaction with residential dining can have an effect on residence hall retention and occupancy.

Financial issues in residential dining mirror those in student housing. As dining programs evolve to provide more choice, flexibility, and convenience for students, the renovation of current dining facilities or the construction of new facilities is a major fiscal issue. Dining facilities built forty years ago were designed to offer a basic food selection (Milius, 1999) and were generally considered utilitarian (McKinnon, 1982). Today, new or renovated dining facilities often offer a "kitchenless" design and stations for branded concepts (Stephens, 1999). As new student housing is built or traditional student housing capacity is expanded, seating capacity in the dining halls is adjusted.

Operational expenses can increase as dining programs extend hours of operation and come up with innovative meal plans that require new technology to administer. Some other financial challenges in residential dining are precipitated by decisions made in the student housing program. For example, when a residence hall is razed and replaced with an apartment complex, the financial consequences for dining are significant. However, just as student housing affects residential dining, the opposite is also true. If the commission structure yields a higher return on board revenues compared to retail sales, the decision to allow residence students to participate in an "all-cash" meal plan (also know as flex dollars or points) can lower commissions without lowering the residential dining operating expenses assigned to the student housing budget.

The Future

The future of student housing finances will likely be reflective of the past. Housing professionals will continue to explore new sources of revenue, discuss the rising cost of utilities, aggressively market to increase occupancy, spend considerable resources on facilities and technology, and move in positive directions to enhance residential life and dining programs. With a strong indication of the freshmen class size increasing for many colleges and universities over the next few years, academic year occupancy trends should remain positive.

Conversely, over the next few years, facilities will be older and, if maintenance is deferred, in dire need of repair and renovation. Discussions will occur more frequently about razing older residence halls (particularly when their construction debt is retired) and replacing them with new facilities. The question will continue to be raised as to whether student housing facilities built in this century should be expected to be functional in forty or fifty years or even longer. If not, college and university construction standards that are not required by code or local, state, or federal regulation may be challenged when building student housing in an attempt to lower construction costs.

Most likely, just as such issues as lead-based paint, ADA legislation, asbestos abatement, and toxic mold were new and major issues for student housing over the past twenty-five years, in the next twenty-five years, student housing facility budgets will be expected to bear further requirements yet to be identified. The renovation of residence halls and apartments will continue to focus on student privacy (rooms and bathrooms), lighting, individual room temperature control, security, storage, and flexible furnishings. The modernization of current facilities will include new or revitalized amenities. Computer labs, for example, will no longer consist of rows of PCs. With wireless technology, comfortable space for group and individual study can be created throughout the facility.

On many campuses, family and partnered housing is at a crossroads. In some cases, the structures were made of wood-framed construction that has outlived its useful life, and fire safety and other code issues constantly call the future of the facilities into question. When considering replacement housing, care must be taken to ensure reasonable rents and flexible designs. Family and partnered housing will clearly be a major issue for many campuses in the years to come.

Residential life programs will undergo significant changes in the future. Costs associated with the modernization of many programs will include new and different levels of staffing, support for a planned integration of faculty and academic programs into the residence environment, and a continued emphasis on the availability of services, programs, and involvement opportunities anywhere and anytime.

Technology will continue to be a significant and ongoing financial issue. Consider that between 1994 and 1998, Internet connectivity in public schools increased from 35 percent to 89 percent (National Center for Education Statistics, 1999). Expectations for student housing service delivery, access, security, building systems, and amenities will involve new and presumably expensive technological advances. The number of students bringing laptops and cellular phones to campus will continue to rise. Overhead costs for auxiliary student housing operations will likely continue to increase to support institutional technology and infrastructure.

Residential dining programs have and will continue to evolve to respond to student lifestyles. Ever-heightening expectations for convenient food service delivery will make traditional dining centers and conventional meal plans obsolete in the decades to come. Costs for facilities, program enhancement, and full-time and student employee wages, recruitment, and retention will remain important financial issues for dining programs.

Student housing programs will face new financial challenges in the future. The overriding issue will be to keep apartment, room, and board rates reasonable so as to ensure the financial success of the student housing program. Student housing departments must be attentive to the college and university mission and strategic directions. Strong relationships should be established with undergraduate and graduate admissions offices, institutional technology, and the physical plant. Student housing finance officers should position the department to fund future expenses. Slightly ramping up the rates each year to support upcoming new debt payments or facilities improvements avoids significant onetime rate increases in the future. Facilities, utilities, repair, maintenance, renovation, and technology will continue to be overriding student housing finance issues in the future. Even while struggling to financially upgrade program components for today's students, the time to prepare for future financial challenges is now.

References

Barr, M. J. "Planning, Managing, and Financing Facilities and Services." In M. J. Barr, M. K. Desler, and Associates, *The Handbook of Student Affairs Administration* (2nd ed.). San Francisco: Jossey-Bass, 2000.

Barr, M. J. *Budget and Financial Management.* San Francisco: Jossey-Bass, 2002.

Brice, C., Kallmyer, S., and Mielke, P. "Budget Planning." *Talking Stick,* 1994, *12*(3), 10–11.

Cowell, W. B., and Gallagher, K. A. "From Sparks to Flames: The Legal Aspects of Fire Safety in Residence Halls." *Journal of College and University Student Housing,* 1998, 27(2), 27–31.

Esteban v. *Central Missouri State College,* 277F. Supp. 649 (W.D. Mo., 1967).

Frederiksen, C. F. "A Brief History of Collegiate Housing." In R. B. Winston Jr., S. Anchors, and Associates, *Student Housing and Residential Life.* San Francisco: Jossey-Bass, 1993.

Gore, V. "The Digital World: So What's Your Strategy?" *Talking Stick,* 2000, *17*(8), 10–13.

Hallenback, D. A. "Business Operations and Facilities Management." In R. B. Winston Jr. and Associates, *Student Housing and Residential Life.* San Francisco: Jossey-Bass, 1993.

Kaplan, W. A., and Lee, B. A. *A Legal Guide for Student Affairs Professionals.* San Francisco: Jossey-Bass, 1997.

McKinnon, W. H. "College Dining Services in the 1980s." *Journal of College and University Student Housing,* 1982, *12*(1), 3–9.

Mielke, P., and Jones, J. "Point of View: New Housing Development Through Partnerships with Private Developers." *Journal of College and University Student Housing,* 2002, *30*(2), 3–10.

Milius, M. "Food Service Master Planning: Preparing for the Next Millennium." *Talking Stick,* 1999, *16*(5), 14–15.

National Center for Education Statistics. *Internet Access in Public Schools and Classrooms, 1994–1998.* Washington, D.C.: U.S. Department of Education, 1999.

National Center for Education Statistics. *Projections of Educational Statistics to 2011.* Washington, D.C.: U.S. Department of Education, 2001.

National Center for Education Statistics. *Digest of Educational Statistics.* Washington, D.C.: U.S. Department of Education, 2002.

Palmer, C. J., and Devine, J. L. "RA Perspectives on Violence in the Residence Halls." *Journal of College and University Student Housing,* 2000, 28(2), 19–24.

Pascarella, E. T., Terenzini, P. T., and Blimling, G. S. "The Impact of Residential Life on Students." In C. C. Schroeder, P. Mable, and Associates, *Realizing the Educational Potential of Residence Halls.* San Francisco: Jossey-Bass, 1994.

Schmidt, J. "Executive Board Responds to RA Unionize Issue." *Talking Stick,* 2002, *19*(7), 4–5.

Schuh, J. H., and Shelley, M. C., II. "External Factors Affecting Room and Board Rates: How Much Influence Does a Housing Director Have?" *Journal of College and University Student Housing,* 2001, *30*(1), 41–47.

Segawa, M. "Are We Missing the Technology Opportunity?" *Journal of College and University Student Housing,* 1999, *28*(1), 3–6.

Stephens, T. "New Millennium Brings New Food Choices to the University of Florida." *Talking Stick,* 1999, *16*(3), 17.

Stoner, K. L. "The Reality of Gap Funding." *Talking Stick,* 2000, *17*(7), 12–17.

Stoner, K. L., and Grimm, J. C. "Facilities for the Future: Where to Begin?" *Talking Stick,* 1996, *14*(4), 12–14.

Strange, C. C., and Banning, J. H. *Educating by Design.* San Francisco: Jossey-Bass, 2001.

U.S. Fire Administration, Federal Emergency Management Agency. "Living with Fire: A Program for Campus and Student Fire Safety." 2002. [http://www.usfa.fema.gov/dhtml/public/campus.cfm].

Weise, G. "Indoor Air Quality." *Talking Stick,* 2001a, *18*(5), 24–26.

Weise, G. "Water Damage, Mold, and Biotoxins: Proper Restoration and Mitigation." *Talking Stick,* 2001b, *19*(1), 6–8.

MARY ANN RYAN is the executive director for campus life at the University of Saint Thomas in Saint Paul, Minnesota. Previously, she was director of housing and residential life at the University of Minnesota, Twin Cities, in Minneapolis.

6

Campus recreation centers, originally quasi-academic facilities, have evolved since the early 1980s: first into campus amenities and then into auxiliary business enterprises. Financial issues affecting campus recreation have changed accordingly and are discussed in this chapter.

Financial Issues in Campus Recreation

Howard Taylor, William F. Canning, Paul Brailsford, Frank Rokosz

This chapter is organized around a number of specific topics concerning financial issues in campus recreation: historical perspective, facilities, business operations, and programs and services. In each area, changes that have occurred in campus recreation departments in recent decades are addressed.

Historical Perspective

To understand present trends, the historical roots of campus recreation must be examined. Funding patterns for campus recreation are related directly to the building of facilities. Facilities were built to meet the demands of an ever-increasing populace engaged in recreational physical activity. Originally, campus recreation served students, faculty, and staff; now, families, alumni, donors, and nonaffiliates also take part. Customers want more and varied activity offerings, which require bigger and more elaborate facilities, all of which requires more money gleaned from various resources.

The first recreational sports facility was opened in 1928 at the University of Michigan. The Intramural Sports Building, which is still in operation, was designed strictly for men's participation in nonvarsity club sports, intramural activities, and physical education. The funding of the department and the cost of the construction were from general funds of the university and the athletic department. Facility construction on campuses throughout the country in the 1930s, 1940s, and 1950s followed that model.

NEW DIRECTIONS FOR STUDENT SERVICES, no. 103, Fall 2003 © Wiley Periodicals, Inc.

The 1960s and 1970s ushered in a new era. The facilities that were constructed still incorporated a physical education academic intent, were built closer to on-campus housing, and were designed for a multipurpose functioning. Both men and women were participating in campus recreation, and modest student fees supported the operation and in some cases a portion of the construction debt. For the first time, faculty, staff, and alumni were also charged a modest user or membership fee. Typically, these facilities had multiple entrances and an academic air, with classrooms, offices, and research labs scattered throughout the building. From a financial point of view, rudimentary services such as towels, lockers, convenience clothing, and guest passes were beginning to be sold, thus creating small income streams. Most new construction took place at major universities with student populations in excess of twenty-five thousand. The large number of students generated sufficient debt retirement capacity through modest student fees.

The 1980s and 1990s witnessed an incredible growth in the building of recreational sport facilities. This growth directly paralleled the expansion of women's involvement in sport and physical activity and society's general interest in fitness. Recreational sport facilities became architectural showcases on campuses. As a consequence, sport and recreational pursuits had become a multibillion-dollar business. University admissions coordinators began to lead tours through wide-open, user-friendly, well-equipped facilities that had become social gathering points on campus. "Admissions offices are pointing to the quality of the out-of-class experiences that the institution has to offer, and one of the top attractions at many institutions is the campus recreational sports facility" (Larry Preo, former director of recreational sports at Marquette and Purdue universities, in Haderlie, 1987, p. 26).

Facilities were in demand by students and others as "quality of life" necessities. All sizes and types of universities and colleges were now planning and constructing huge new recreation centers and using them as student recruitment and retention tools. Increased student fees were necessary to cover the cost of the debt incurred to build these facilities; consequently, higher fees were charged for membership. Members began requesting additional services and programs as they came to recognize the importance of a healthier lifestyle. The size of recreational sport staffs and budgets mushroomed. Recreational services, programs, and membership were perceived as making increased contributions to the well-being of the entire campus community.

The design of facilities began to change from large-box, fortress-type structures with multiple entrances and few windows in activity spaces to facilities with single-entry-and-egress front doors that were beacons of welcome to the community. Large windows displayed the inner activities, connecting the inside activity to the outside environment. Campus recreation departments were, of necessity, becoming entrepreneurial entities within the campus administrative structures of athletics, student affairs, business operations, or academic programs.

Clearly, the emphasis on healthy lifestyles and the construction of modern recreation centers have changed the direction of campus recreation and the role of the recreation professional (Combes, 1988). Presently, the construction of new facilities is returning to major universities that built facilities in the 1960s and 1970s. Those dated facilities no longer meet the new programming and service demands. Projects that range from $60 to $80 million are the norm, and some that top $100 million are being planned. Financially, colleges and universities have a huge investment in these facilities, which must be managed professionally and maintained superbly. Recreational sport facilities are now destination points on campus, designed with a clublike atmosphere. These days, campus recreation is a business that requires the staff to be well grounded in financial issues.

Facilities

The need to be 100 percent self-supporting with respect to both debt service and operating costs has driven the evolution of campus recreation centers. Accordingly, the manner in which recreation improvements are funded also has evolved. As recreation facilities became more clearly differentiated from academic facilities, traditional fundraising and state allocations came to be viewed as inappropriate for the funding of recreation facilities, and hence student-fee-based financing of recreation facilities became increasingly common. Starting in the 1980s, additional revenues were sought to supplement student fee revenue, which led to the sale of nonstudent memberships as well as auxiliary services and programs.

Nonstudent fee revenues, often labeled "other income," is difficult to project accurately because it is highly speculative to project how many people will purchase memberships, participate in programs, and use services that are designed to generate additional revenues. It is this element of uncertainty, coupled with the actual importance of "other income" to the feasibility of building and operating a modern campus recreation center, that has led many colleges to approach the planning of these projects through the application of sophisticated analysis.

While maximizing "other income" is critically important, most contemporary recreation centers derive 70 to 85 percent of their revenues from mandatory student fees. This makes the process of determining the appropriate fee level and policy of critical importance. Early in the planning process, the method of implementing the fee must be chosen. A student referendum should be held only if necessary. Referendums take time, add cost, and introduce an element of risk. It is desirable to hold a referendum only if a statutory requirement exists, if there is a preexisting commitment by the administration to the student body, or for political reasons (for example, senior administrators might be reluctant to be perceived as responsible for increasing the cost of attending a public institution).

In any case, it is essential to involve students early in the planning process, gauge and document student interest and preferences using focus groups and surveys, and communicate with students often and consistently through the student government and media. If the process of sizing the fee feels right to the students, the new fee is likely to be supported widely, regardless of whether a referendum is held or not. A referendum should never be a "fishing expedition" but rather should be a confirmation of support that already exists.

The tremendous growth in the number of recreational facilities that has transpired is due in large part to the institutions' readiness and ability to manage debt. It has been made possible by the students' willingness to tax themselves by passing referendums or supporting projects by covering the cost of construction and operation of these facilities. Planning for the financing of these contemporary campus recreation centers is no longer a simple exercise; it requires the application of rigorous analysis. Funding a contemporary recreation facility requires the implementation of concepts and terms typically associated with the funding of commercial facilities.

It is necessary to define a few terms in order to continue with this discussion. *Debt capacity* is the amount of debt that an organization can manage. At many state universities, this is an amount established by state statute. *Net operating income* (NOI) is defined as operating revenues minus operating expenses; it represents the amount of money available to be "leveraged" into debt, as well as that required to fund major maintenance and replacement reserve accounts. *Leverage* is the extent to which the NOI can support debt, and it is a function of the debt term, interest rate, and debt coverage ratio. *Debt coverage* is a measure of operating risk and is expressed as a ratio of the NOI to the annual debt payment. Debt coverage is expressed as a ratio such as 1.2:1, which, in this case, means that there must be $1.20 of NOI for every $1.00 of debt payment. It is the tool that underwriters use to protect the bondholders from unrealized financial performance. Accordingly, riskier projects require higher debt coverage ratios. Typically, debt coverage ratios applied to campus recreation centers that are supported by student fees fall between 1.15:1 and 1.25:1. This topic is critical because the modern campus recreation department and its programs are closely tied to the strategic value of the modern recreation facility.

Basically, debt capacity is affected by the relationship of the debt term, debt coverage, and interest rates. The debt capacity of the recreation facility grows as interest rates go down, debt term is extended, and the debt coverage ratio goes down. When considering the debt coverage ratio most appropriate for the project's risk level, it is important to realize that high-quality projects typically perform better with respect to generating other income. It may be less risky from a revenue perspective to increase debt capacity through a reduction in the debt coverage than it is to reduce the building quality to be able to increase the debt coverage ratio. These issues must be considered in determining the appropriateness of a given leveraging strategy.

The rapid pace at which modern recreation centers are being built is the result of compelling mission-based objectives that recreation centers help support—educational outcomes, enrollment management plans, and a range of other institutional values and commitments. Clearly, it is in the interest of every college and university to select an aggressive leveraging strategy that is in line with its ability to manage the associated risk. It is also important, while developing the financial planning for a new facility, to plan for long-term capital projects and repair and replacement costs. If possible, it is often advantageous to the long-term success of the project to deal with such matters on the level of the individual project as opposed to dealing with it as a part of the larger university plan.

Often little thought is given to the proposed recreation center's operating paradigm. The operating paradigm determines the primary revenue-generating strategy that in turn determines levels of service and staffing that are reflected in the financial projections. Operating paradigms (further detailed in our discussion of business operations) fall into three categories: traditional, facility-driven, and program-driven models. The traditional model emphasizes intramurals, sport clubs, and open recreation for students. The facility-driven model generates revenues through facility rentals and events. The program-driven model maximizes nonstudent membership opportunities and delivers a broad menu of programs and services.

It is critically important that the operating paradigm, financial projections, and building program for the facility be reconciled carefully. For example, a facility might have the capacity to support a large number of employee and alumni memberships or generate substantial revenues through facility rentals and events. But because members expect unlimited access to facilities during normal operating hours, attempts to maximize rental and event activity are likely to interrupt member access to facilities. Such interruptions will diminish the value of the membership and limit the facility's ability to maintain the projected membership base. Many other examples of revenue reconciliation issues could be cited, but the point is that the uncertainty of generating the projected revenues must be understood well before incurring the facility construction debt.

Reconciling revenue projections with the limitations of the facility and the membership market is also critically important. Understanding accessibility of the facility is essential to developing accurate membership revenue projections. Will the facility be visible from the campus edge? Will parking or convenient public transportation be available? Does a substantial portion of the targeted population, such as alumni, live or work near the facility? Considering that overcrowding is one of the most frequently cited reasons people terminate memberships, does the facility have the capacity to accommodate the projected memberships?

The quality of the facility must also be consistent with the financial projections. Members will pay more to use a high-quality, well-equipped, well-staffed facility that offers top-notch programs and services. So the question becomes, by spending more on quality, can one make more in the long run?

Another issue relative to facility planning relates to a needs assessment. Unfortunately, some facilities have been built too small or without certain critical features. In recent years, schools such as Ohio State and the University of Illinois have taken the approach of conducting a thorough assessment of the recreational interests of their clientele before developing a building plan.

Business Operations

Any campus recreation department with facility management responsibilities is required to manage multimillion-dollar budgets. Therefore, sound fiscal management and controls are necessary. As facilities are designed and programs developed, the operational paradigm must be part of the planning process. As mentioned earlier, recreational sport facilities fall into three basic paradigms: traditional, facility-driven, and program-driven models.

Traditional Model. The emphasis in the traditional model is on the student-based programs of intramurals and club sports. Typically, this operational paradigm is funded through student fees. Facilities and operations are heavily subsidized by the general fund or other sources. The emphasis is not on creating income but on meeting student demand at low cost. A traditional program usually has a small staff, and the major expenses of utilities, custodial and maintenance services, and personnel are not within the recreational sports director's sphere of responsibility.

Facility-Driven Model. This facility management operation places the emphasis on renting the facilities and associated services to "outside" groups to generate income. The income is designed to subsidize the operations for "regular" facility users. Facilities that are shared between different campus entities typically fall within this paradigm. Regular users have to be flexible in their usage patterns to accommodate changes in the rental schedule. Staffs, again, are typically small, and operational budgets are funded from other sources.

Program-Driven Model. The basis for the program-driven model comes from a fee that is levied on the students plus memberships sold to part-time students, continuing students, faculty and staff, retirees, alumni, donors, nonaffiliates, and families of such. Large income streams are generated by memberships, but that income is only as reliable as the attractiveness of the facility, programs, and services provided. This paradigm places great pressure on the facility staff to provide quality experiences for the membership.

Services and Amenities. Services and amenities are a key to the over-all experience for each user who enters a facility. Food service is a good example of a feature found in the modern recreational facility. This could be a bar serving salads, smoothies, and juices; a coffee shop; or a full-service grill. For the most part, food operations are leased to a campus or local food professional, and they become yet another source of income for the facility. Lounges are also essential. Recreational sport facilities have become a social gathering point on campus. Areas designed for sitting, conversation, watch-ing big-screen televisions, computer use, and passive recreation are very popular. Small retail operations exist in most facilities, generating additional income. Equipment items, such as swimming goggles, shirts, and racquet-balls, are sold at the equipment room counter or in a full-scale on-site sport-ing goods shop.

As the business of recreational sports has changed over the years, so have the responsibilities of the professional staffs. Personnel must now be more than programmers and trainers of officials. Professionals experienced in mar-keting, event management, customer service, facility management and main-tenance, personnel management, information technology services, and financial management are required to maintain the contemporary recreational sport business operation.

Recreational facilities are typically open twelve to sixteen hours a day, but some are operating twenty-four hours a day, seven days a week. This requires not only a highly trained full-time professional staff but also one significantly augmented with part-time student workers. Recreational sport departments are now among the largest student employers on campus. That makes it essential that departments have professionals with student devel-opment and leadership backgrounds.

Because many recreational sports departments generate large amounts of cash daily, having a secure cash-handling system is essential (Combes, 1988). The modern recreational sports department must follow approved business practices and procedures to maintain credibility and efficient oper-ations. Controls can be either preventive or detective in nature. A basic system of control involves segregation of duties, documentation, double-checking, and reconciling. Segregation of duties means that an individual should have responsibility for only one of the money-handling transaction components. Documentation means that every area and repeatable task must be properly recorded. Double-checking is a safeguard that ensures accuracy. Reconciling is the simple comparison of one set of information with another to verify accuracy. Because of the increased complexity of these business operations and the volume of cash transactions being man-aged, point-of-sale systems and other computerized accounting programs must be employed to properly track this information (Ross, 1988).

Repair and Renovation. As noted earlier, campus recreation build-ings can be very expensive to build and maintain and to outfit with com-plex equipment. For the facilities to be attractive to users—be they students, faculty, staff, renters, or whoever else—a facility and its equipment need to be in pristine condition. As a consequence, as soon as a facility is open, plans need to be developed for the repair and replacement of equipment and the maintenance of the facility. It is inescapable that swimming pools may leak, lockers will rust, wooden floors need refinishing, exercise equipment breaks down or becomes obsolete, and so on. Consequently, substantial expenses can be incurred in bringing the facility up to the condition expected by users. That requires a long-term financial plan and a dedicated revenue stream to make sure that as the facility ages, it can still meet the needs and expectations of users.

Programs

The expansion of facilities and funding opportunities in recent years has led to an expansion of programs offered. While many programs are funded primarily through student fees, additional revenue-generating concepts have been developed to support membership-based recreational sports departments (Jamieson, 1988; Glover and Goepper, 1990). Generally, these revenue-generating concepts do not make a profit.

The departmental mission guides programming decisions and program pricing. Some programs are offered at a loss or on a break-even basis. This is done to provide a necessary program that may serve a special need. Other programs may generate significant excess revenues, and these help support the department's ability to offer other programs. Some institutions have taken the approach of including access to most programs through one universal membership fee. Others have established a basic membership fee and then charge an additional fee for participation in each specific program.

Programs can benefit from basic marketing, packaging, delivery, and assessment strategies. Marketing strategies help maximize participation, thereby increasing revenue. "Package deals" are usually successful, offering the user a bargain through enrollment in multiple programs. Providing quality delivery through efficient office and registration processes can help maximize revenues while contributing to a positive image (Bulfin, 1988). By employing regular and targeted assessments, the recreational sports department can change and adapt to the needs of members.

The following are some of the programs offered to generate additional revenue.

Sport Clubs. Sport clubs provide students with many opportunities to enjoy and experience a wide variety of sports and other participatory activities. Cleave (1994, p. 30) states that "because of their organizational structure and financial autonomy, sport clubs can be a cost-effective way for an institution to provide a wide diversity of programs to serve the varied needs of the student body."

Funding for sport clubs plays a significant role in the recreation department (Cleave, 1994) and can be distributed in several ways, depending on

the form of governance used to oversee clubs. One involves a direct allocation from student fees that comes directly through student government
accounts. Another has recreational sports departments receiving a lump
sum of money, which is divided up among the clubs at the department's discretion or by a committee of peers. Some departments set aside a pool of
funds in what they call an "excellence fund" to support clubs that qualify
for regional or national competition.

Allocated funds often do not adequately provide for the needs of the
club; additional revenue is therefore needed. Clubs generate that additional
revenue through membership dues, donations, and fundraising. It is
extremely important that clubs be given training in fundraising techniques.
This can be handled by the university's foundation or fundraising arm.

Because funding is coming from both university and outside sources,
the question of whether sport clubs should have an account established
within the institution or with an outside financial organization often arises.
Having university accounts helps establish better controls and is the
preferred approach. Without proper controls, clubs can get into trouble
through the inappropriate use of funds (Cleave, 1994). Accounts should be
established such that dual signatures are required for expenditures and
withdrawals.

Another issue affecting clubs involves what happens to equipment that
is purchased with club funds year after year. How is it accounted for and
inventoried? How does the equipment change hands as the student leadership of the club changes? Should the recreational sports department handle
inventory and control? Are students held accountable for equipment that
they don't return at the end of each school year? What items should be considered personal and paid for by the student participants, and which items
can be transferred each year to the new members of the club? These issues
need to be covered in operating policies for club sports and explained to
student participants on an annual basis so that there is no confusion at the
end of the academic year when equipment has to be accounted for and
inventoried.

Financial issues with sport clubs are affected by a school's view of governance. Often this has been guided by the school's philosophy of risk management and liability concerns. Some schools believe that by keeping their
distance, they are insulated from risk. Others believe that they should
be more actively involved to better manage the risk. The trend seems to be
toward closer controls and governance of sport clubs.

Finally, the cost of club sports can be substantial, depending on the
nature of the sport, the equipment required, the venue for the sport, and
travel costs. In some sports, team members coach each other, while in others, a part-time or full-time coach is hired. Some sports, such as soccer,
require little in the way of equipment, while others, such as crew, require
very expensive accoutrements such as racing shells. A well-marked field will
suffice as the playing site for some sports, whereas the costs of venues for

other sports—the rental of ice time for hockey, for example—can be substantial. In some sports, the teams compete with local colleges and universities or even local athletic clubs. In other sports, travel can be very expensive—for example, the American Collegiate Hockey Association holds a national tournament each year involving teams from all over the country. A plan needs to be developed to underwrite the costs of the various club sports that an institution may offer, and in many cases, the athletes themselves will need to be involved in raising funds to support the costs of operating their club team.

Team Challenge, Experiential Education, and Leadership Training. This area of programming is growing at many schools around the country. It generally involves the use of a low- or high-ropes course for the development of team building, problem solving, communication, and leadership in a particular group. These programs can generate a great deal of revenue (in some cases, more than $50,000 per year). Kent Bunker, the director at Oklahoma State University, which operates Camp Redlands, and Richard Romero, at the University of Arizona, both indicate that their ropes course program generates a significant amount of revenue each year. The University of Arizona paid for its facility within the first two years of operation. Numerous campus groups benefit from this program, and many off-campus groups and corporations are looking to incorporate these programs as part of their own employee training and development. Because these facilities are usually separate from indoor recreational facilities, expanding their use does not generally have a negative impact on regular users.

Intramural Sports. Intramural sports has been one of the foundational campus recreation programs over the years, and it provides many opportunities to offset the cost of operation. It is common practice to charge nonrefundable entry fees. Also, many programs have developed some type of forfeit fee, deposit, or fine. Teams are assessed a fine or lose a deposit if they fail to show up for a scheduled game.

One of the interesting things that has developed in recent years involves corporate sponsorships. Many programs have thousands of contacts with students each year, providing opportunities for businesses and corporations to advertise their products and services. Sponsorships can entail cash support, equipment donations, provision of awards, and product giveaways.

Group Fitness and Noncredit Instruction. This area includes such group fitness and instructional classes as aerobics, yoga, kickboxing, Pilates, racquetball, and tennis. There are several ways of charging for these programs. One is to charge a general fee that allows the participant to attend any program on the schedule. Another is to charge a class fee for the entire semester, which allows the student to attend only that class. Still another is to charge a daily class fee, which is paid each time the student attends a class. Combinations of these fee payment systems are not unusual.

Class enrollment fees can also depend on who teaches them—students or outside, contracted professionals. Outside instructors cost more, but they may be more experienced and offer higher-quality instruction.

Recent trends that have had a negative effect in group fitness enrollment include self-training and individualized exercise programs. There has been an increasing interest in yoga, tai chi, Pilates, NIA, and other mind-body activities.

Personal Training, Physical Assessment, and Massage. For people who desire one-on-one attention, the services of licensed personal trainers and massage therapists could be offered. These can be contracted services, rental agreements, or fee-based programs, depending on how the program or service is staffed. Other special services that can generate revenue include body composition analysis, nutrition counseling, and fitness testing and assessments.

Camps and Children's Programs. There is significant demand for youth recreation opportunities and summer camp programs. This area provides a tremendous opportunity to generate a great deal of income and profit. The program can involve activities such as sport-specific camps, general summer camps, swimming lessons for kids, and game activities. Parents are looking for safe and convenient programs for their children, particularly in the summer. Most camp programs offer either half-day or full-day programming, and they run one or two weeks. Some schools administer overnight camps that use university housing and provide meals for the campers. Camps can be considered a form of early recruitment of future students, and they can generate revenue in excess of $50,000 per year.

The recreational sports department at the University of California in Berkeley has developed a youth program that is significantly supported by a fundraising component similar to those used by athletic departments. The Bear Backer Youth campaign supports the camp and programs offered. Donors receive priority sign-up for youth programs, and donations in the first year totaled over $35,000, according to the university's director of recreational sports. The university also decided to offer donors special memberships for use of the recreational facilities; at $50 each, the memberships have generated an additional $150,000.

Outdoor Pursuits and Trips. These programs generate revenue through the provision of guided camping and adventure trips. Outdoor recreation generates great interest, but sustaining high quality in the type of equipment purchased and the maintenance of equipment is costly. Transportation is expensive, and it involves safety risks. Some programs have looked at outside travel agencies to administer the outdoor trips. Some examples include chartered ski trips, river rafting, canoeing, and twenty-four-hour turnaround trips to accessible attractions.

Services

Facility rentals, pro shops, and various rental services are often part of the portfolio of services provided by recreational sports. Each is discussed in detail in this section.

Facility Rentals. Campus recreational facilities are usually large, multipurpose spaces that are easily marketed to potential renters (Canning, 1988), and the revenue generated can be significant (in excess of $100,000 per year). Most schools look to rent space during low-use times so that regular users are not displaced. Arizona State University has a three-tiered approach to rental charges. Student groups are charged the lowest rate, other university groups are charged a slightly higher rate, and the highest rate is charged to off-campus groups. Typically, off-campus groups must show proof of insurance or should list the university as an additional insured.

To ensure that groups are serious about renting the space, it is usually prudent to charge a deposit that is forfeited if the group cancels. Also, securing advance payment for the rental is a way to prevent postrental collection problems. These arrangements should be agreed to in writing or, even better, should involve a detailed formal rental agreement. The contract should hold the group financially responsible for damage to facilities or equipment. Language should be included that provides for late charges in the event the group does not relinquish or vacate the rental space when specified. It is also important to plan for the cost of cleaning facilities when large rentals expire. Ancillary benefits from a rental program can be had through the exposure of the facilities to various campus and community groups (Canning, 1988). Further, student employees can staff the rentals, providing them with additional working hours.

Pro Shops. Pro shops and merchandise sales can be profitable and will provide a steady stream of revenue, according to John Sweeney (1988), recreation director at Northern Illinois University. He suggests a variety of issues to be considered in order to keep the pro shop profitable. One issue that affects the success of a pro shop is its location in the facility and the ease of access to sporting goods in the community. The ability to sell items at competitive prices is influenced by the cost of overhead and volume-purchasing capability. Sweeney expresses a concern with maintaining high levels of inventory that may be necessary to compete for sales of items such as shoes and racquets. Another problem that must be solved is maintaining inventory control and deterring shoplifting and employee theft. Some schools have had success operating mini pro shops that involve front-office staff in the sale of merchandise.

Typically, these mini pro shops sell necessary items such as soap, shampoo, socks, weight gloves, locks, and tennis balls, racquetballs, and table tennis balls. These are items that users may forget to bring with them and need immediately in order to participate. This approach avoids the high cost of maintaining inventory on items such as racquets, shoes, and clothing. These mini pro shops generate revenue while serving the immediate needs of their users. In certain markets, it is very difficult to compete with nearby sporting good stores, department stores, and discount stores on many items. Often they are able to offer a wider selection at prices lower than the recreation center can actually purchase the items. Each school must assess its ability to compete for the sale of merchandise in its particular market.

Outdoor and Sports Equipment Rentals and Locker and Towel Services. A significant amount of equipment can be used in the recreational facility. Some programs incorporate the cost and maintenance of checkout equipment into the membership fee. Others make equipment available at an additional fee. Accurate checkout and return procedures must be established to maintain inventory control. Many programs have expanded to incorporate outdoor adventure centers into their operation. The purchase and maintenance of this rental equipment can be very expensive. It is helpful to use this equipment in conjunction with the outdoor trip program.

Locker and towel services also require sound management. If the cost of towel service is incorporated into the membership fee, it is considered a value-added benefit to the membership and is priced accordingly. If fees are charged separately for this service, it can be optional and will generate revenue accordingly. There are pros and cons to both approaches, based in part on the cost of providing the service to all or part of the membership. Many members will repeatedly renew this type of service as long as they continue to use the facility. Often demand for lockers exceeds availability. A successful locker and towel program must efficiently deal with locker and towel checkout, cleanup, security controls, and much more.

Concluding Observations

Significant changes have occurred in campus recreation in recent decades. What were once departmental budgets expressed in thousands of dollars have grown into programs with multimillion-dollar budgets and elaborate recreation centers. Recreation facilities and programs have become strategic assets for colleges and universities, helping them meet their objectives and missions, such as the recruitment and retention of students. This has led to an improvement in the campus environment and has positioned campus recreation at the forefront of the university experience.

References

Bulfin, D. "Registration Process: Help or Hindrance?" *NIRSA Journal,* 1988, *21*(3), 33–38.

Canning, W. F. "Producing Income Through the Rental of Facilities." *NIRSA Journal,* 1988, *13*(1), 43–47.

Cleave, S. "Sport Clubs: More Than a Solution to Shrinking Dollars and Growing Demands." *NIRSA Journal,* 1994, *18*(3), 31–33.

Combes, M. "Daily Cash Controls: Step One for the Rec-Business Person." *NIRSA Journal,* 1988, *13*(1), 33–35.

Glover, R., and Goepper, C. "Financing the Future." *NIRSA Journal,* 1990, *14*(2), 28–30.

Haderlie, B. "Influences of Campus Recreation Programs and Facilities on Student Recruitment and Retention." *NIRSA Journal,* 1987, *11*(3), 24–27.

Jamieson, L. "Trends in Financing Recreational Sports." *NIRSA Journal,* 1988, *12*(3), 16–19.

Ross, C. M. "Computer-Based Accounting in Recreational Sports." *NIRSA Journal,* 1988, *12*(3), 35–37.

Sweeney, J. "Pro-Shops Serving an Ace." *NIRSA Journal,* 1988, *12*(3), 31–32.

HOWARD TAYLOR is the director of campus recreation at Arizona State University.

WILLIAM F. CANNING is the principal of recreational sports at the University of Michigan and president of Centers, LLC.

PAUL BRAILSFORD is the CEO of Brailsford & Dunlavey and a principal with Centers, LLC.

FRANK ROKOSZ is an associate professor in the Kinesiology and Sport Studies Department at Wichita State University.

7

This chapter provides an overview of strategies that can be used to demonstrate accountability in financial issues in student affairs.

Selected Accountability and Assessment Issues

John H. Schuh

This issue of *New Directions for Student Services* concludes with some thoughts about how one might go about demonstrating accountability and effectiveness in financial management issues. This topic seems to become more complex with each passing day. It used to be that if the budget was kept in balance and that some planning was done to renovate facilities and replace worn equipment, everything was fine. But the financial environment has changed dramatically over the past few years, and precious little evidence suggests that it will change in the foreseeable future.

This chapter provides a concise conceptual framework for looking at accountability issues in student affairs finance. In it, I make some suggestions for developing indicators that will help interpret the financial situation of the various units in student affairs to the various constituencies they serve. I will then suggest some questions to guide an evaluation of financial issues in student affairs units.

Conceptual Framework

In the main, what one attempts to do in looking at accountability issues in finance is to answer this question: Are our resources being well spent? The question may seen simple, but the answer can be complex. Just looking at this question from the perspective of potential clients, the answer can be yes, no, or maybe. For example, the person who never uses the campus recreation center might respond that all expenditures on recreation are a waste of resources. At the other end of the continuum is the backyard and intramural athlete who spends some time in the gymnasium working out each day. For this person, monies are well spent because the facility and its programs are an important part of the college experience. Given the wide spectrum of potential responses, the individuals responsible for demonstrating accountability in the financial matters of student affairs have to strike a defendable position and provide data that support it.

Kennedy, Moran, and Upcraft (2001, p. 176) identified three key questions to ask in assessing the effectiveness of expenditures in student affairs:

1. How does the service or program contribute to the institution's mission?
2. In what direction is the institution headed?
3. What are the institution's budget policies?

These three questions provide an excellent framework for analyzing expenditures and in some respects also provide a wonderful way of thinking about student affairs on a given campus from a strategic point of view. Not all campuses need all units that one might find in a student affairs division. For example, at a residential college that serves students of traditional age, a facility that is developed to provide care for the children of students is probably unnecessary because few, if any, of the students will have child care responsibilities. By contrast, a traditional residential campus, particularly if it is in a fairly small community, might have to develop some services more typical of an urban institution enrolling primarily part-time students over the age of thirty.

So the first issue, that of examining how various services, programs, and activities (referred to hereafter as "the unit") contribute to the institution's mission, needs to be studied with great care. Centrality, meaning that the unit contributes to the heart of the institution's mission, is crucial. The more peripheral a unit becomes, the greater its chances of being perceived as unimportant and a potential target for budget reduction or elimination.

Looking at the direction in which an institution is headed provides additional insight into the centrality of a unit. As an institution changes its enrollment mix (for example, adding more graduate students, recruiting more international students, eliminating an on-campus residence hall living requirement for first-year students, and so on), units in student affairs will be affected. On the one hand, if an institution were to attract more international students, for example, services for these students might have to be added. On the other hand, elimination of the residency requirement for first-year students could have implications for certain campus programs.

Finally, Kennedy, Moran, and Upcraft (2001) looked at the question of an institution's budget policies. In Chapter Two, Claar and Scott pointed out some of the differences between public and private institutions. Beyond that, the extent to which student affairs units are to be self-sustaining or supported by the general fund is an important variable in evaluating student affairs finance. What is the institution's philosophy about developing partnerships with private organizations? Many student affairs units can be operated through outsourcing (see Dietz and Enchelmayer, 2001), and in some cases that is the direction that institutions have taken. In other circumstances, the institution's philosophy is such that outsourcing is kept to a minimum.

Certainly, when there is a change in the senior officer of the institution or the senior business officer, it is time to understand what changes, if any, will be brought to the executive table. Will things continue as they have been, or will a change in leadership signal a philosophical change in how accountability is measured? These questions and others will help guide issues of accountability in student affairs finance.

Use of Benchmarks and Other Indicators

One of the most useful tools in demonstrating accountability in financial matters can be the use of benchmarks and other indicators. Taylor and Massy (1996) studied nearly one thousand colleges and identified approximately one hundred key performance indicators. These were broad measures of institutional performance, ranging from the percentage of alumni who were donors to the percentage of students with college work-study jobs. Taylor and Massy provide excellent examples of how benchmarks can be used to measure performance.

More specific benchmarks have been discussed in other situations. For example, Secor (2002) described how benchmarks were used at Penn State University when it joined the Big Ten Conference. Barak and Kniker (2002) reported on how governing boards use benchmarking in their work. So examples abound of how benchmarks can be used in various ways in higher education. Benchmarking has direct applications to student affairs units and can take a variety of forms.

Forms of Benchmarks. Lee Upcraft and I identified three forms of benchmarking that have salience for this discussion (Upcraft and Schuh, 1996, citing Spendolini). First, internal benchmarking could be used to compare costs between units within the student affairs division. Suppose that staffing costs are an issue on campus. What does it cost per student to staff the counseling center compared with the health center? What does it cost on a per-student-served basis to staff an advising center in one college (say, liberal arts and sciences) compared with another (business or engineering) on campus? These questions and others would make sense for someone engaged in internal benchmarking.

Competitive benchmarking is used to draw comparisons with an institution's direct competitors. Mosier and Schwarzmueller (2002) have described how housing officers in partnership with Educational Benchmarking Inc. have developed this form of benchmarking to inform the work of housing officers and residence educators. Assuming similar missions, what does institution X spend per student on campus recreation compared with institution Y located across the state? How much does it cost to run the student activities office on a per-student basis compared with an institution on the other side of the city? The key here, we pointed out, is to "choose institutions, functions, and services that are comparable to your own" (Upcraft and Schuh, 1996, p. 241).

Finally, we identified functional or generic benchmarking. This is used to draw comparisons with organizations that may not be your competitors and may not even be in higher education. How long do patients wait to be seen at the local immediate-care clinic compared to the campus health service? What does a parent pay per hour for care at the campus child care center compared to a similar service off campus?

Developing Benchmarks. Virtually every unit in student affairs should be able to develop a list of financial benchmarks, assuming that such benchmarks are not already in place on campus at the time the decision is made to begin benchmarking. Among the benchmarks that could be developed are the following:

The annual cost per student for the unit each year (determined by dividing the total budget by total enrollment)

The annual cost per student per staff member in the unit (determined by dividing the total staffing budget by total enrollment)

The cost per student for a specific program (determined by dividing the total cost of the program by the number of attendees)

The annual cost per student for major renovation projects (determined by dividing the cost of the project by total enrollment)

The annualized cost per student of debt for a facility (determined by dividing total outstanding debt by the number of students served by the unit on an annual basis)

The percentage of the unit budget compared with the total student affairs budget (determined by dividing the unit budget by the total student affairs division budget)

The percentage of the student affairs budget within the context of the total institutional budget (determined by diving the student affairs budget by the institutional budget)

The cost of the use of a service each time it is used by a client (determined by dividing total expenditures by the total number of visits by client; an example might be the total budget of a counseling center divided by the total number of clients seen at the counseling center on an annual basis)

Cost for each visit by a client to a campus service compared to cost for a visit at a local service (for example, comparing the cost for each visit at the campus counseling center with the cost of a visit to the local mental health agency)

Increase in costs on a year-by-year basis compared to increases in various indices, such as the Higher Education Price Index or the Consumer Price Index (determined by comparing the percentage increase year over year with the change in the index of choice)

Comparison of the per-student cost of the unit with similar institutions
Comparison of the per-student cost of the student affairs budget of the institution with peers

This simple list can be modified to apply to a variety of student affairs units or even the entire student affairs division. What is important is that if one chooses to develop benchmarks, that they need to be meaningful in the institution's unique context.

Determining Benefits. After calculating benchmarks or other forms of analysis of the cost of various services, activities, and programs, the next step is to determine their benefits. At times, this determination is relative in that the unit might be part of the larger package of what it means to be a part of the institution. That an institution has a bookstore in and of itself will probably not be the determining factor in a prospective student's decision to attend, but the absence of a bookstore could be a negative in the mind of a prospect. Kennedy, Moran, and Upcraft (2001) identify a number of benefits that need to be determined in the evaluation of cost effectiveness. Their work provides the basis for the following discussion. It is very important to emphasize, however, that data are necessary to make the following arguments. My view is that institutions have moved far beyond the philosophical in assessing the benefits of various activities. Students affairs units are well advised to gather ample empirical evidence in making their case. Arguments stemming from a purely philosophical stance are no longer persuasive and have little relevance in the contemporary economic environment.

Because students are the primary clients of colleges and universities, the direct benefits to them of offering specific programs, services, and activities must be determined. Among the elements to be considered are the quality of the unit (defined previously as programs, activities, and services), the convenience of the unit, and what the absence of the unit would mean. Generating data along these lines can be as simple as conducting focus groups with students to determine their perceptions of the unit under consideration. An important element of various units in student affairs is what the absence of them would mean in a crisis. What would it mean to a campus if a measles outbreak occurred and a health service was not available (Schuh, 1983)? What would happen in a time of crisis not to have a counseling center (Schuh and Shipton, 1985)? How would the campus community be affected if no one were available to address the developmental needs of students if residence hall staff did not exist? The picture becomes clearer with these examples: an institution would be taking a major risk and potentially leaving itself open to liability if these units did not exist. Moreover, what would it mean to the life of the institution if students who needed these services had to secure them on their own? The answers to these questions begin to get at the value, both tangible and intangible, of these units.

The benefits to staff of various units also need to be calculated. Such units as food service, campus recreation, and counseling and health services often play an important role in providing services to staff. What would it mean to the staff members of the institution if they had to make various arrangements privately, ranging from planning a banquet for a departmental guest to arranging for an immediate intervention on the part of the counseling center in the case of a student issue?

Various units in student affairs also contribute to the general benefit of the campus. Graduation and retention rates are a source of ongoing concern for most institutions, and many units contribute directly to the persistence and retention of students (Pascarella and Terenzini, 1991). Having data (see Pike, Schroeder, and Berry, 1997, for example) that directly support the conclusion that various units contribute to persistence and graduation rates moves units from peripheral status at an institution to one of centrality.

Considering Alternatives. The final step in this process of determining cost effectiveness and evaluating financial expenditures is to consider various alternatives. Kennedy, Moran, and Upcraft (2001) provide five questions that guide this thinking:

1. *Should the unit be eliminated?* This question gets at the viability of the unit. Does it contribute to the mission of the institution? If the case to sustain the unit cannot be made, perhaps it needs to be eliminated. A change in institutional mission, for example, could lead to a decision of this type.

2. *Could the unit be provided for less money?* Back in the days of the military draft and widespread military service, many campuses had large offices that provided services for veterans. As the size of the military has contracted and service has become voluntary, the need for these offices has diminished. To maintain a veterans' affairs office of the same size as in 1970 could potentially be a waste of resources. That explains why on many campuses these offices were eliminated.

3. *Could a unit be downsized?* Short of eliminating a unit, could it be downsized by eliminating weekend or evening service? Could a service be offered just in the mornings or just in the afternoons? Usage patterns need to be studied and services provided at times when students and other clients are most likely to use the services provided. For example, if students could order an unofficial online transcript for themselves at any time, would there be need to provide a staff member to provide that service from 8:00 A.M. to 5:00 P.M. each day? If technology can be used effectively, it may help in the downsizing of a unit without diminishing service to students.

4. *Could the unit be outsourced?* The decision to outsource has both philosophical and economic dimensions to it. Nevertheless, there are many examples where outsourcing has resulted in excellent services to students at a manageable cost. While the possibility of outsourcing certain units can cause some angst for campus administrators contemplating such a decision,

in the long run, forming a relationship with an off-campus partner is an appropriate course of action.

5. *Can the unit be funded differently?* With increasing pressure on the general funds of most campuses (defined as tuition and state appropriations for state-supported institutions and tuition and fees for independent institutions), one strategy is to find a different way to fund various units. Fees are charged for various services once were provided without additional charge. This is not inappropriate, given that the fees are often charged for services that some, but not all, students use, such as charging for prescriptions at the health service or for tickets to major sporting events, parking passes, and the like. In effect, what the institution is saying to the potential user is this: "We can provide this additional service to you, but an additional cost comes with it. So you will have to pay your share of the cost to enjoy its benefit." In difficult financial times, this strategy is common and is likely to become even more common in the future.

Conclusion

This chapter has provided a cursory overview of ways to evaluate financial decisions in a student affairs division. Very few people get into student affairs work because they want to manage large amounts of money and be responsible for substantial resources (buildings, equipment, and so on). Nevertheless, in challenging economic times, student affairs leaders must understand the financial dynamics of their situation, for if they do not, someone else will. It is essential that student affairs leaders think about measuring financial performance and success and consider the financial dimensions of their various units that comprise student affairs. Armed with this information as well as what specific institutions provide, tomorrow's student affairs leaders will be able to make a solid economic case for the good work they do.

References

Barak, R. J., and Kniker, C. R. "Benchmarking by State Higher Education Boards." In B. E. Bender and J. H. Schuh (eds.), *Using Benchmarking to Inform Practice in Higher Education.* New Directions for Higher Education, no. 118. San Francisco: Jossey-Bass, 2002.

Dietz, L. H., and Enchelmayer, E. J. (eds.). *Developing External Partnerships for Cost-Effective, Enhanced Service.* New Directions for Student Services, no. 96. San Francisco: Jossey-Bass, 2001.

Kennedy, K., Moran, L., and Upcraft, M. L. "Assessing Cost Effectiveness." In J. H. Schuh and M. L. Upcraft (eds.), *Assessment in Student Affairs: An Applications Manual.* San Francisco: Jossey-Bass, 2001.

Mosier, R. E., and Schwarzmueller, G. J. "Benchmarking in Student Affairs." In B. E. Bender and J. H. Schuh (eds.), *Using Benchmarking to Inform Practice in Higher Education.* New Directions for Higher Education, no. 118. San Francisco: Jossey-Bass, 2002.

Pascarella, E. T., and Terenzini, P. T. *How College Affects Students: Findings and Insights from Twenty Years of Research.* San Francisco: Jossey-Bass, 1991.

Pike, G. R., Schroeder, C. C., and Berry, T. R. "Enhancing the Educational Impact of Residence Halls: The Relationship Between Residential Learning Communities and First-Year College Experiences and Persistence." *Journal of College Student Development*, 1997, *38*, 609–621

Schuh, J. H. "When the Measles Come to College: Implications for Student Affairs Administrators." *College Student Affairs Journal*, 1983, *5*(2), 32–36.

Schuh, J. H., and Shipton, W. C. "The Residence Hall Resource Team: Collaboration in Counseling Activities." *Journal of Counseling and Development*, 1985, *63*, 380–381.

Secor, R. "Penn State Joins the Big Ten and Learns to Benchmark." In B. E. Bender and J. H. Schuh (eds.), *Using Benchmarking to Inform Practice in Higher Education.* New Directions for Higher Education, no. 118. San Francisco: Jossey-Bass, 2002.

Taylor, B. E., and Massy, W. F. *Strategic Indicators for Higher Education.* Princeton, N.J.: Peterson, 1996.

Upcraft, M. L., and Schuh, J. H. *Assessment in Student Affairs: A Guide for Practitioners.* San Francisco: Jossey-Bass, 1996.

JOHN H. SCHUH is distinguished professor and chair of the department of educational leadership and policy studies at Iowa State University. He was a student affairs practitioner for twenty-seven years.

INDEX

Accountability: benchmarking for demonstrating, 5; benchmarks for assessing, 89–92; conceptual framework for examining, 87–93; student affairs finance trend toward, 5
ADA (Americans with Disabilities Act), 5, 62
Alcohol abuse prevention programs, 50
Alexander, F. K., 12
Alpha State University, 21–24
America Reads program (University of Illinois at Urbana-Champaign), 14
Annual Survey of Counseling Center Directors, 42
Askew, P. E., 14
Assessment: benchmarks for, 89–92; conceptual framework for examining, 87–93; student affairs finance trends regarding, 5; three key questions for student affairs, 88
Association of College and University Housing Officers (2002 conference), 66
Association for University and College Counseling Center Directors, 54

Banning, J. H., 65
Barak, R. J., 4, 89
Barr, M. J., 4, 22, 24, 27, 67
Bear Backer Youth campaign (UC Berkeley), 83
Benchmarks: assessing accountability using, 89; defining, 5; development of, 90–91; three kinds of, 89–90
Bender, B. E., 5
Berdahl, R. O., 4
Bernal, E. M., 3
Bishop, J. B., 42
Blackburn Institute (University of Alabama), 14
Blimling, G. S., 5
Brailsford, P., 2, 73, 86
Brice, C., 62
Bridge to Hope program (University of Hawaii), 14
Budgeting: Alpha State University case study on, 21–24; comparing public/private institutions, 24–28; development process in private institutions,

18; development process in public institutions, 20–21; differences in public/private institutions, 26–28; implications for student affairs, 28–29; John Dewey College case study on, 18–20; similarities in public/private institutions, 24–26
Bunker, K., 82
Butts, P., 31

Cabrera, A. F., 3
Camp Redlands (Oklahoma State University), 82
Campus recreation business operations: facility-driven model of, 78; program-driven model of, 78; repair and renovation expenses of, 79–80; services and amenities offered by, 79; traditional model of, 78
Campus recreation financial issues: business operations and, 78–80; facilities as, 75–78; historical perspective on, 73–75; programs as, 80–83; reconciling operations, financial projects, and building program, 77; reconciling revenue, quality of facility, and needs assessment, 77–78; self-supporting requirement as, 75; services as, 83–85; terminology of, 76–77
Campus recreation financial sources: facility rentals, 84; outdoor and sports equipment rentals/services, 85; pro shops, 84–85
Campus recreation programs: camps and children's programs, 83; considering alternatives to, 92–93; determining benefits of, 91–92; group fitness/noncredit instruction, 82–83; intramural sports, 82; outdoor pursuits/trips, 83; overview of, 80; personal training, physical assessment, and massage, 83; ropes course, 82; sport clubs, 80–82
Campus Security Act (1990), 5
Canning, W. F., 2, 73, 86
CDC (Centers for Disease Control and Prevention), 50
Center for Campus Free Speech, 35
Central Missouri State College, Esteban v., 66

95

Back Issue/Subscription Order Form

Copy or detach and send to:
Jossey-Bass, A Wiley Company, 989 Market Street, San Francisco CA 94103-1741

Call or fax toll-free: Phone 888-378-2537 6:30AM – 3PM PST; Fax 888-481-2665

Back Issues: Please send me the following issues at $27 each
(Important: please include ISBN number with your order.)

_____

_____

_____

$ _____   Total for single issues

$ _____   SHIPPING CHARGES: SURFACE   Domestic Canadian
                                    First Item $5.00 $6.00
                                    Each Add'l Item $3.00 $1.50
               For next-day and second-day delivery rates, call the number listed above.

Subscriptions   Please __ start __ renew my subscription to *New Directions for Student Services* for the year 2_____ at the following rate:

U.S.	__ Individual $70	__ Institutional $145
Canada	__ Individual $70	__ Institutional $185
All Others	__ Individual $94	__ Institutional $219
Online Subscription		__ Institutional $145

**For more information about online subscriptions visit
www.interscience.wiley.com**

$ _____   Total single issues and subscriptions (Add appropriate sales tax
               for your state for single issue orders. No sales tax for U.S.
               subscriptions. Canadian residents, add GST for subscriptions and
               single issues.)

__Payment enclosed (U.S. check or money order only)
__VISA __ MC __ AmEx __ Card #_____Exp.Date_____

Signature _____ Day Phone _____
__Bill Me (U.S. institutional orders only. Purchase order required.)

Purchase order # _____
                 Federal Tax ID13559302   GST 89102 8052

Name _____

Address _____

_____

Phone _____ E-mail _____

For more information about Jossey-Bass, visit our Web site at www.josseybass.com

PROMOTION CODE ND03

SS98   **The Art and Practical Wisdom of Student Affairs Leadership**
Jon Dalton, Marguerite McClinton
This issue collects reflections, stories, and advice about the art and practice
of student affairs leadership. Ten senior student affairs leaders were asked to
maintain a journal and record their personal reflections on practical wisdom
they have gained in the profession. The authors looked inside themselves to
provide personal and candid insight into the convictions and values that
have guided them in their work and lives.
ISBN: 0-7879-6340-2

SS97   **Working with Asian American College Students**
*Marylu K. McEwen, Corinne Maekawa Kodama, Alvin N. Alvarez, Sunny Lee,
Christopher T. H. Liang*
Highlights the diversity of Asian American college students, analyzes the
"model minority" myth and the stereotype of the "perfidious foreigner," and
points out the need to consider the racial identity and racial consciousness
of Asian American students. Various authors propose a model of Asian
American student development, address issues of Asian Americans who are
at educational risk, discuss the importance of integration and collaboration
between student affairs and Asian American studies programs, and offer
strategies for developing socially conscious Asian American student leaders.
ISBN: 0-7879-6292-9S

SS96   **Developing External Partnerships for Cost-Effective, Enhanced Service**
Larry H. Dietz, Ernest J. Enchelmayer
Offers a variety of models for the enhancement of services through external
partnership, including on- and off-campus collaboration with public and
private entities. Explores the challenges student affairs professionals face
when determining how to meet a particular constituency's needs in the most
cost-effective and efficient manner.
ISBN: 0-7879-5788-7

SS95   **The Implications of Student Spirituality for Student Affairs Practice**
Margaret A. Jablonski
Provides student affairs professionals and others on college campuses with
information and guidance about including spirituality in student life
programs and in the curriculum of preparation programs. Explores the role
that faith and spirit play in individual and group development on our
campuses. Models of leadership, staff development, and graduate education
itself are all examined from the context of spirituality.
ISBN: 0-7879-5787-9

SS94   **Consumers, Adversaries, and Partners: Working with the Families of
Undergraduates**
Bonnie V. Daniel, B. Ross Scott
Presents effective strategies for student services professionals to collaborate
and coordinate in creating a consistent message of engagement for the
families of today's college students. Parents, stepparents, grandparents, and
others who serve as guardians of college students are challenging
administrators to address their concerns in a variety of areas, including
admissions and financial aid processes, orientation programs, residence life,
and alumni and development activities.
ISBN: 0-7879-5786-0

SS93   **Student Services for Athletes**
        Mary F. Howard-Hamilton, Sherry K. Watt
        Explores a full range of issues, including the ongoing impact of Title IX, the
        integration of student athletes into on-campus residence halls, the college
        experience for minority athletes, and the expansion of opportunities for
        women athletes.
        ISBN: 0-7879-5757-7

SS92   **Leadership and Management Issues for a New Century**
        Dudley B. Woodard Jr., Patrick Love, Susan R. Komives
        Examines new approaches to learning requiring a new kind of leadership,
        and describes the important role played by student affairs professionals in
        creating and sustaining learning communities. Explores how changes in
        students will affect student affairs work, outlines new dimensions of student
        affairs capital, and details the importance of active and collaborative
        leadership for creating a more flexible structure to handle future challenges.
        ISBN: 0-7879-5445-4

SS91   **Serving Students with Disabilities**
        Holley A. Belch
        Explores the critical role that community and dignity play in creating a
        meaningful educational experience for students with disabilities and shows how
        to help these students gain meaningful access and full participation in campus
        activities. Addresses such common concerns as fulfilling legal requirements and
        overcoming architectural barriers, as well as effective approaches to recruitment
        and retention, strategies for career and academic advising, and the impact of
        financial resources on funding programs and services.
        ISBN: 0-7879-5444-6

SS90   **Powerful Programming for Student Learning: Approaches That Make a
        Difference**
        Debora L. Liddell, Jon P. Lund
        Assists student affairs professionals as they plan, implement, and evaluate
        their educational interventions on college and university campuses. Details
        each step of program assessment, planning, implementation, and outcome
        evaluation. Explains the importance of collaborating with faculty and others,
        illustrating several types of programming partnerships with four brief case
        studies, and examines the significant partnership aspects that led to
        programming success.
        ISBN: 0-7879-5443-8

SS89   **The Role Student Aid Plays in Enrollment Management**
        Michael D. Coomes
        Discusses the political and cultural contexts that influence decisions about
        student aid and enrollment management, the special enrollment
        management challenges facing independent colleges, and some alternative
        methods for financing a college education. Provides a review of the research
        on the impact of student aid on recruitment and retention,
        recommendations for ethical enrollment planning, and a list of resources for
        enrollment planners, researchers, and policymakers.
        ISBN: 0-7879-5378-4

SS88   Understanding and Applying Cognitive Development Theory
        Patrick G. Love, Victoria L. Guthrie
        Reviews five theories of the cognitive development of college students and
        explores the applications of those theories for student affairs practice. These
        theories shed light on gender-related patterns of knowing and reasoning;
        interpersonal, cultural, and emotional influences on cognitive development;
        and people's methods of approaching complex issues and defending what
        they believe.
        ISBN: 0-7879-4870-5

SS87   Creating Successful Partnerships Between Academic and Student Affairs
        John H. Schuh, Elizabeth J. Whitt
        Presents case studies of academic and student affairs partnerships that have
        been successfully put into practice at a variety of institutions, in areas such as
        service learning, the core curriculum, and residential learning communities.
        ISBN: 0-7879-4869-1

SS86   Beyond Borders: How International Developments Are Changing
        International Affairs Practice
        Diane L. Cooper, James M. Lancaster
        Assesses the impact of international trends and developments on the student
        affairs profession and offers practical suggestions for developing the
        knowledge and skills requisite for a global future. Explains how to recruit
        and support international students and provide valuable information on
        student and staff exchange programs. Presents case studies from student
        affairs professionals in Mexico, Germany, and Hong Kong, highlighting the
        global student affairs issues that transcend national borders.
        ISBN: 0-7879-4868-3

SS85   Student Affairs Research, Evaluation, and Assessment: Structure and
        Practice in an Era of Change
        Gary D. Malaney
        Describes how student affairs and faculty can collaborate to create an agenda
        for student-related research; reviews technological aids for collecting and
        analyzing data; and discusses how student affairs researchers can make their
        role more vital to the campus by expanding into policy analysis and
        information brokering.
        ISBN: 0-7879-4216-2

SS84   Strategies for Staff Development: Personal and Professional Education in
        the 21st Century
        William A. Bryan, Robert A. Schwartz
        Offers a range of strategies for recruiting, retaining, and developing an
        educated, energetic, and motivated student affairs staff. Examines a
        performance-based approach to human resource development, the impact of
        supervisors and mentors on those entering and advancing in the field, and
        the influence of behavioral style on professional development.
        ISBN: 0-7879-4455-6

SS83   **Responding to the New Affirmative Action Climate**
        Donald D. Gehring
        Explores how to achieve an economically, ethnically, spiritually, and
        culturally diverse student body while complying with confusing and
        sometimes conflicting laws and judicial pronouncements. Clarifies the law as
        it relates to affirmative action in admissions and financial aid; discusses
        alternatives to race-based methods for achieving diversity; and reports on a
        national study of student affairs programs that have successfully used
        affirmative action.
        ISBN: 0-7879-4215-4

SS82   **Beyond Law and Policy: Reaffirming the Role of Student Affairs**
        Diane L. Cooper, James M. Lancaster
        Examines higher education's apparent over-reliance on policy and shows how
        we can redirect our attention to the ethical and developmental issues that
        underlie the undergraduate experience. Discusses how learning communities
        and creeds can help achieve balance between policy and personal responsibility;
        how to deal with student misconduct in a way that both reduces the risk of
        litigation and furthers student development; and how to promote
        multiculturalism without compromising individual rights and freedoms.
        ISBN: 0-7879-4214-6

SS80   **Helping African American Men Succeed in College**
        Michael J. Cuyjet
        Offers practical strategies, proven models and programs, and the
        essential theoretical grounding necessary for nurturing and retaining
        African American male students. Explores ways to make classroom
        environments more supportive; the benefits of mentoring initiatives;
        the opportunities for leadership development on a predominantly white
        campus; and more.
        ISBN: 0-7879-9883-4

SS78   **Using Technology to Promote Student Learning: Opportunities for Today
        and Tomorrow**
        Catherine McHugh Engstrom, Kevin W. Kruger
        Explores critical issues that have developed with the increased use of
        technology, including strategic planning process needs, financial and
        infrastructure issues, policy implications, curricular issues for student affairs
        graduate programs, and ethical considerations.
        ISBN: 0-7879-9858-3

SS76   **Total Quality Management: Applying Its Principles to Student Affairs**
        William A. Bryan
        Provides balanced coverage of information for student affairs professionals
        regarding total quality management principles and discusses issues
        surrounding their use. Provides examples of the application of these
        principles and techniques in student affairs settings.
        ISBN: 0-7879-9932-6

NEW DIRECTIONS FOR STUDENT SERVICES
IS NOW AVAILABLE ONLINE AT WILEY INTERSCIENCE

What is Wiley InterScience?

Wiley InterScience is the dynamic online content service from John Wiley & Sons delivering the full text of over 300 leading scientific, technical, medical, and professional journals, plus major reference works, the acclaimed *Current Protocols* laboratory manuals, and even the full text of select Wiley print books online.

What are some special features of Wiley InterScience?

Wiley InterScience Alerts is a service that delivers table of contents via e-mail for any journal available on Wiley InterScience as soon as a new issue is published online.
Early View is Wiley's exclusive service presenting individual articles online as soon as they are ready, even before the release of the compiled print issue. These articles are complete, peer-reviewed, and citable.
CrossRef is the innovative multi-publisher reference linking system enabling readers to move seamlessly from a reference in a journal article to the cited publication, typically located on a different server and published by a different publisher.

How can I access Wiley InterScience?

Visit http://www.interscience.wiley.com

Guest Users can browse Wiley InterScience for unrestricted access to journal Tables of Contents and Article Abstracts, or use the powerful search engine.
Registered Users are provided with a *Personal Home Page* to store and manage customized alerts, searches, and links to favorite journals and articles. Additionally, Registered Users can view free Online Sample Issues and preview selected material from major reference works.
Licensed Customers are entitled to access full-text journal articles in PDF, with select journals also offering full-text HTML.

How do I become an Authorized User?

Authorized Users are individuals authorized by a paying Customer to have access to the journals in Wiley InterScience. For example, a university that subscribes to Wiley journals is considered to be the Customer. Faculty, staff and students authorized by the university to have access to those journals in Wiley InterScience are Authorized Users. Users should contact their Library for information on which Wiley journals they have access to in Wiley InterScience.

ASK YOUR INSTITUTION ABOUT WILEY INTERSCIENCE TODAY!